Patterns of Sound SERIES

The Choral Approach to

Sight-Singing

for 3-Part Mixed Voices

VOLUME I

I0808906

by
Emily Crocker
and
Joyce Eilers

- *Starts from square one, assuming no previous training*
- *Quick results, easy-to-use*
- *Logical organization and sequencing*
- *Combinable exercises develop rhythmic and melodic independence*
- *3-Part Mixed Songs (a cappella and accompanied) help relate the process of sight-reading to "real music"*
- *Success for all students!*

HAL•LEONARD® CORPORATION
7777 W. BLUEMOUND RD. P.O. BOX 13819 MILWAUKEE, WI 53213

THE CHORAL APPROACH TO SIGHT-SINGING, VOLUME I

TABLE OF CONTENTS

	Teacher	Singer
Teacher's Guide	3	
What Is 3-Part Mixed?		
Course Overview		
How To Use This Book		
Introduction	5	3
Rhythm - Let's Begin	6	4
Singing Exercise I	7	5
Singing Exercise II	8	6
*SONG 1: A New Horizon	9	7
Rests - Silent Beats	12	10
Singing Exercise III	13	11
Singing Exercise IV	14	12
Three Parts Together	15	13
*SONG 2: Oh My! What A Morning	16	14
The Pitch Ladder (Tonic Chord)	18	16
Pitch Ladder Practice	19	17
*SONG 3: Let Your Voice Be Heard	20	18
C - A New Key	23	21
Key Of C Exercises	24	22
New Patterns (Eighth Notes)	25	23
SONG 4: The Fox And The Grapes	26	24
Eighth Note Practice	27	25
Short Songs - Key of C	28	26
*SONG 5: Three Bluebirds	29	27
New Patterns - 3/4 and 2/4	33	31
3/4 and 2/4 Practice (Key of G)	34	32
3/4 and 2/4 Practice (Key of C)	35	33
SONG 6: Old Joe Atkinson	36	34
SONG 7: Characters	37	35
Warm-Ups And Tune-Ups (Key of G)	38	36
Warm-Ups And Tune-Ups (Key of C)	39	37
Ties	40	38
More Practice With Ties	41	39
Slurs	42	40
More Practice With Slurs	43	41
Dotted Notes	44	42
Dotted Note Practice	45	43
SONG 8: America	46	44
SONG 9: Hold On!	47	45
*SONG 10: Swing Low, Sweet Chariot	48	46
F - A New Key	52	50
More Tune-Ups (Key of F)	53	51
Key Of F Exercises	54	52
SONG 11: Auld Lang Syne	55	53
*SONG 12: Old England	56	54
How To Find Do	60	58
Key Of B Flat	61	59
Key Of D	62	60
Key Of A	63	61
Key Of E Flat	64	62
Key Of A Flat	65	63
Preview Of Volume II	66	64
Terms And Symbols Glossary	67	

*Accompanied Song

TEACHER'S GUIDE

What Is Three-Part Mixed?

One of the interesting developments in middle school and junior high music education programs in the past few years has been the evolution of the three-part mixed choir. In many cases there has been an enrollment drop among boys due to scheduling difficulties and other conflicts. Often, the few boys who do enroll are an interesting combination of totally unchanged voices, totally changed voices, and some voices which are in the process of changing. Yet, these boys, though few in number, have a social need to sit together and sing the same part.

Regular SAB music is often too low for the unchanged and changing voices, and the result is a large gap between the alto and the baritone part. SSA music is totally out of range for the changed voices and often has feminine qualities. Two-part music doesn't make sufficient use of the talent in the upper voices and neither Part I or Part II can accommodate the changing voice.

The answer for many choirs has been Three-Part Mixed music, which uses a **compromise range** for Part III. It is notated in bass clef to stress the masculine aspect of the music, although it is usually within the range of many female altos. The range is very limited:

with an occasionally optional note above or below. Limited as it is, it is not ideal, as it is too high for the totally changed voices, too low for the totally unchanged voices, but it is generally just right for those voices which are enroute. While it is not perfect, it is possible.

Understandably, any choral conductor would prefer to work with an SATB group, but if the group has few boys, or if they don't have the adequate range or experience for SATB music, three-part mixed music can be the answer. Additionally the singers can gain the confidence and experience to eventually move on to more challenging material.

If you have found the need to use this voicing, **THE CHORAL APPROACH TO SIGHT-SINGING** will help you teach your students to sight-read. If your students have used **PATTERNS OF SOUND Sight-Singing Course For Young Singers** by Joyce Eilers and Emily Crocker, **THE CHORAL APPROACH TO SIGHT-SINGING** is a logical extension for the middle school/junior high singer whose voice is beginning to mature. If, however, your students are beginning sight-singers, **THE CHORAL APPROACH TO SIGHT-SINGING** starts from square one, assuming no previous training. It's logical design and easy-to-use format help produce quick results. Three-part harmony is introduced through combinable exercises, which produce rhythmic and melodic independence.

One of the important features of this method is the use of "real songs" which help relate the process of sight-reading to "real music." These songs, both a cappella and accompanied, occur at certain points throughout the book, and serve to reinforce the musical concepts that have been introduced in the exercises. These songs become "intrinsic rewards" and are usually anticipated with great enthusiasm by the students.

Your students' skills will grow by leaps and bounds. Success breeds succeeds - for all students, not just the gifted few. The potential for real musicality in your young singers is tremendous and this method is designed to help them achieve it. We hope you will find the path to musical literacy to be equally satisfying for both you and your students.

Course Overview

Volume I: Rhythmic concepts include quarter, half, dotted half, whole notes and rests; eighth notes and rests; dotted quarter/eighth patterns; 4/4, 3/4, 2/4 meters; ties and slurs. **Melodic concepts** include songs and exercises in the major keys of G, C, F, B flat, D, A, E flat, A flat; how to find "do" in any key. **Harmonic concepts** include introduction to 3-part singing, combinable exercises, 12 songs (a cappella and accompanied) chord progressions (including an optional bass part) and interval practice in the I, IV, and V chords.

Volume II: Rhythmic concepts include syncopation, sixteenth notes, dotted rhythms, 6/8. **Melodic concepts** include more challenging melodic exercises with larger intervals and more variety; accidentals, minor keys, and modulations. **Harmonic concepts** include more a cappella and accompanied songs (many with an optional bass part) and minor key chord progressions.

THE CHORAL APPROACH TO SIGHT-SINGING has been developed using the rhythm syllables popularized by Kodaly and Orff teachers, and the movable "do" system of melodic syllables. Other counting and melodic reading methods may be used, if you wish, but the key is consistency and regular practice.

While the essence of this method is to avoid overloading the student with a lot of musical vocabulary and labels, the teacher is encouraged to be flexible and answer the questions that arise, even if it means jumping ahead briefly. These "teachable moments" will surely save time in the long run.

How To Use This Book

THE CHORAL APPROACH TO SIGHT-SINGING can be part of a successful sight-singing program if you will consider several basic principles:

1. Boys are intelligent and willing, and they can be the foundation of a successful choir. They can and will learn to sight-read quickly and well.

2. Rhythm accounts for more than 50% of the difficulty in sight-reading, so this method separates the concepts of rhythm and pitch. Always emphasize and reinforce rhythmic comprehension. Go beyond understanding to habit.

3. Young male and female singers need to be equally fluent in treble and bass clef notation in order to be aware of how their part relates to the whole. Encourage them to read the clefs interchangeably in the combinable exercises (in their own register). It will be more appropriate to stay within their own parts on actual songs.

4. The comprehensive teaching suggestions, lesson plans, and other helpful hints which are included in the Teacher's Edition are based on an "average" situation. Differences in age, maturity, sophistication, as well as ethnic and regional differences will necessitate adjustments. Teachers are encouraged to adapt as necessary for their own individual situations.

5. Limit the time for sight-reading, even if the students are successful and feeling extra confident. 10-15 minutes daily should usually be sufficient.

6. Remember the value of repetition. Go back and review previously covered material for extra reinforcement and confidence building.

7. Try to keep all students involved at all times, either by studying or practicing their own part silently, or by singing each other's part. Remember, if you don't find things for them to do with their minds and mouths, they will!

8. Always be musical, whether working with songs or exercises.

9. Stress to the students, that you will do everything in your power to not waste their time, and expect the same in return.

10. In learning your "other" music for concert performance, help students to transfer their sight-singing skills to other situations. In addition, supplement this method with songs that the students are able to sight-read all or portions of.

Introduction

Notes On The Staff

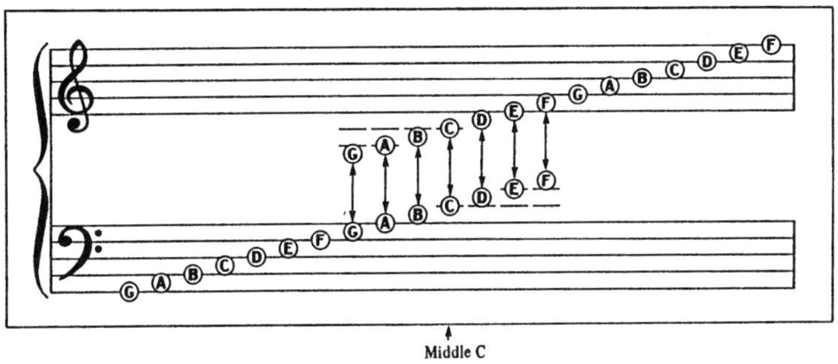

Notes On The Keyboard

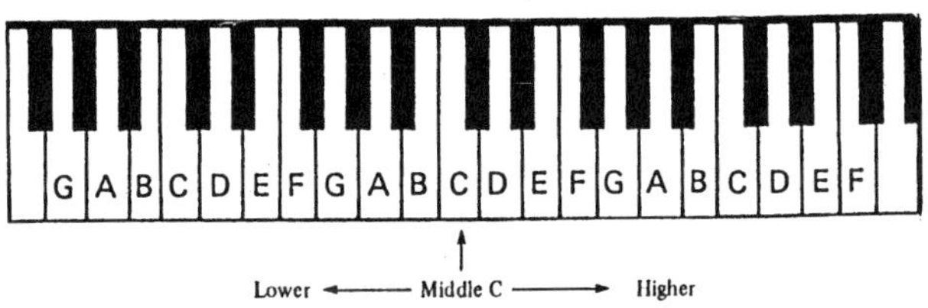

Higher voices usually sing notes on the treble staff (above middle C).

Lower voices usually sing notes on the bass staff (below middle C).

Some notes (indicated by arrows above) can be written on either staff.

Introduction

Teaching Suggestions:

Concepts:

- 𝄞 Treble Clef
- 𝄢 Bass Clef
- Location and names of notes on the staff and keyboard

Directions:

- Use the piano keyboard to help the students find middle C.
- Show middle C as it appears in the bass and treble clefs and emphasize that it is the same note.
- Help students become familiar with the letter names (absolute pitch names) of the notes on the staff. Stress the importance of knowing both bass clef and treble clef no matter what part they usually sing.

NOTE: Encourage the students to discover their own vocal range. They may find it interesting to keep a record of their vocal range on an individual or group chart, especially as their voices develop.

Rhythm - Let's Begin

Teaching Suggestions:

Concepts:

- See, understand, and use:
  ♩ 𝅗𝅥 𝅗𝅥. 𝅝
- Gain understanding of measure and four bar phrase through use not discussion.
- Understand the importance of the steady beat, and how it holds everything together.

Directions:

- Count each line.
- Count each line in random order without stopping.
- Count lines in random order.
- Make up new combinations.

NOTE: While other counting methods may be adapted to work with this course, the neutral syllable "ta" was selected for uniformity.

It is not necessary to go into all the quantitative relationships at this point. However, teachers are to be encouraged to be flexible and to answer students' questions as they arise. Taking advantage of the "teachable moment" saves time in the long run.

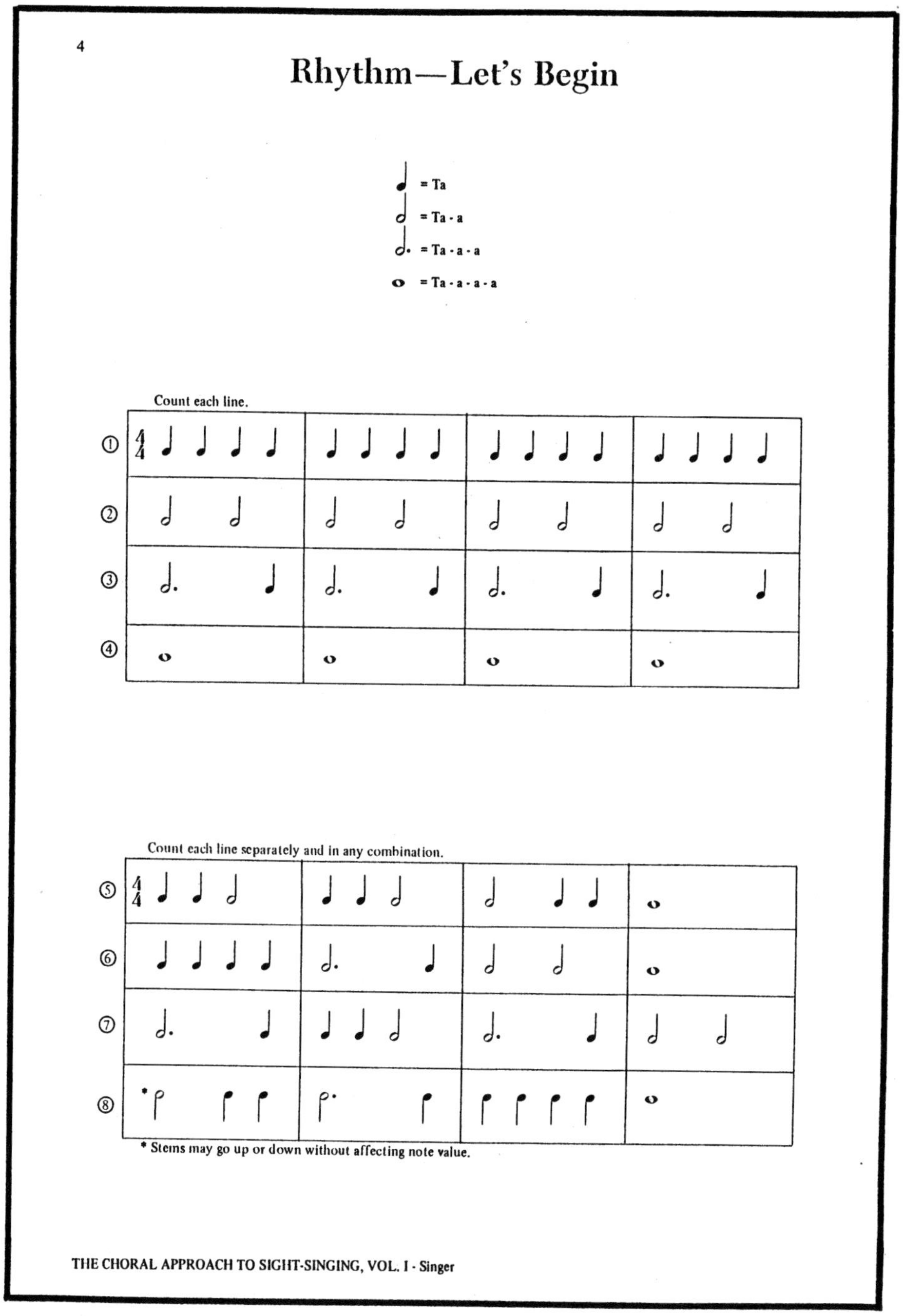

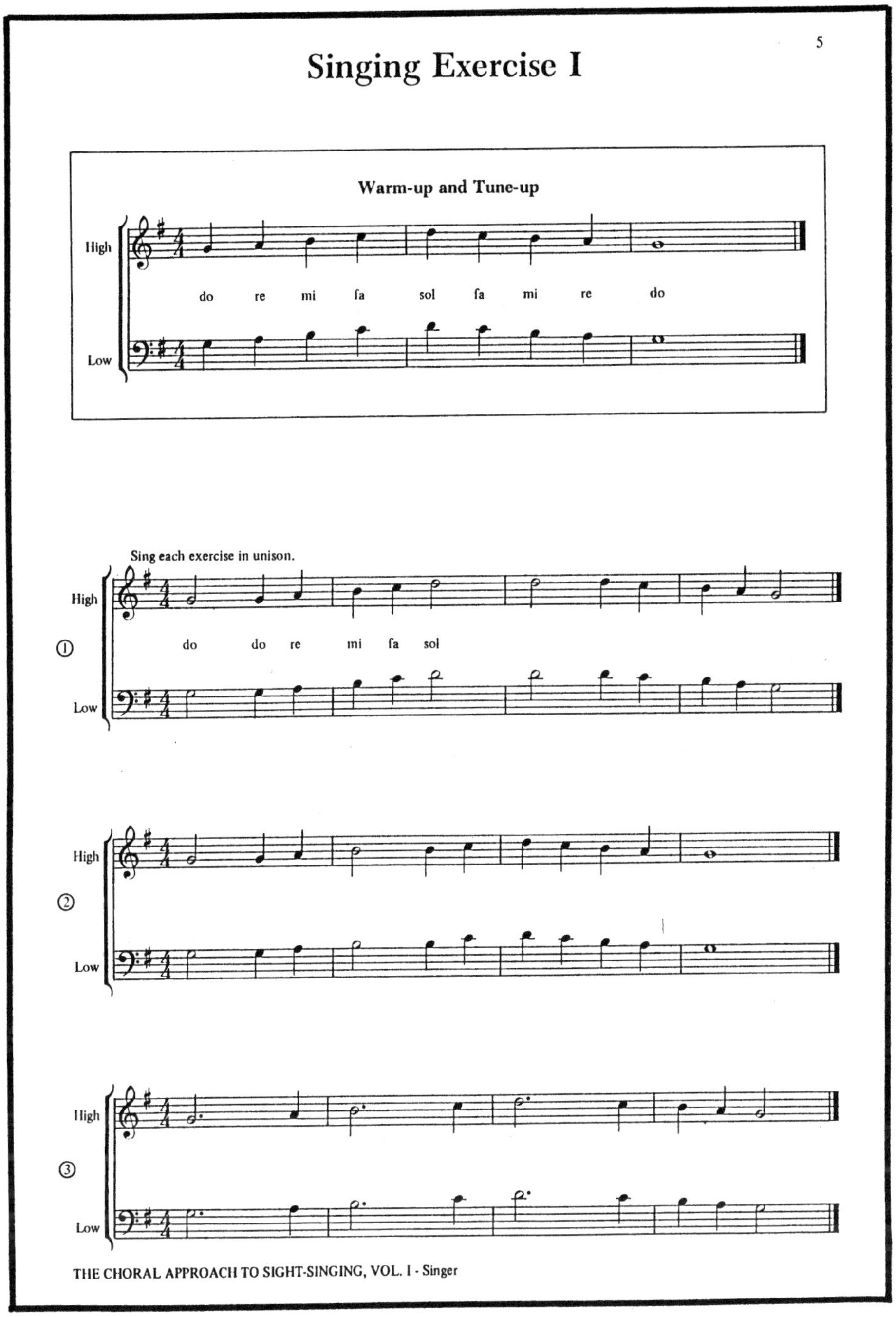

Singing Exercise I

Teaching Suggestions:

Concepts:

- Steady Beat
- Rhythm:

- Pitch:

- Students will learn to recognize that unison pitches will appear to be different because of the treble and bass clefs, but they sound the same, although an octave apart.
- Bracketed Staves (Lines)

Directions:

- Say the rhythm.
- Say the pitch syllables (or letter names) in rhythm.
- Sing the exercises. If the students have little experience in singing, the teacher may sing with them the first time through as a model, but after that, they should sing alone.
- Give the students the chance to correct their own mistakes. If they are still making the same mistakes after the second time, isolate the errors, correct them, and repeat.
- Beware of flatting on "mi." For acoustical reasons, this pitch is vulnerable.

Singing Exercise II

Teaching Suggestions:

Concepts:

- Rhythm:

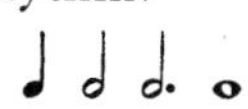

- Steady Beat
- Pitch:

- Non-bracketed lines (staves), 2-line exercises, double bar
- Unisons that appear different because of clef differences.

Directions:

- Count each exercise, being sure to continue through the second line to the double bar.
- Say the pitch syllables in rhythm.
- Sing the pitch syllables in rhythm.
- Sing the exercises in unison and in any combination.
- Point out that in these two-line exercises, the singers should sing until they reach the double bar.

OPTIONAL: Say and sing letter names of the exercises to reinforce letter name recognition, so the students will recognize unisons immediately, in spite of clef differences.

NOTE: Even though the boys will be singing the lower voice lines, boys and girls should be aware of each other's clef, so as to learn note relationships.

A New Horizon

Teaching Suggestions:

An important feature of this method is the inclusion of actual songs, both accompanied and a cappella, which will help relate the process of sight-reading to "real music." Each song has been written so as to use only the rhythmic and melodic concepts which have been introduced up to that point.

Concepts:

- Rhythm:

- Pitch: (Key of G)

- Harmony: Unison
- Form: Alike and Different
- Accompaniment: A visual introduction to the relationship between "singing lines" and "piano lines," and the piano introduction.
- Other:

’ (breath mark)

poco rit.

(See glossary for a full explanation.)

NOTE: This song makes use of a whole rest in the vocals both in the introduction and in measure 20. While rests are not introduced until page 10 (Singer's Edition), you may want to give a brief explanation.

(Teaching suggestions continued on next page)

A New Horizon (continued)

Directions:

It is important to establish good habits and procedures in the first stages of learning to sight-read, primarily concerning the separation of rhythm and pitch in the preparation for singing. In the beginning stages, follow this sequence carefully and do not make a habit of skipping steps until much later after the singers are very secure and confident sight-readers.

- Locate the singer's parts, high voices and low voices. Locate the piano part.
- Speak the rhythm of the vocal parts, keeping a steady beat throughout.
- Speak the pitch syllables (solfege) in rhythm, keeping a steady beat. Alternate: speak the letter names in rhythm.
- Find the places in the song that seem to be the same. Are they exactly the same? How are they different?
- Establish the pitch and sing in solfege, keeping a steady beat.
- Repeat. Allow the students to correct their own mistakes, unless a passage is missed repeatedly. In that case, isolate and correct.
- Sing in solfege with accompaniment.

(Cont. on next page)

- Sing with words a cappella. (Note: this is a big step!)
- Sing with words and piano accompaniment.

NOTE: This is the basic sequence in preparing to sight-read a song. In future songs, the instructions may not be as detailed as these. Refer back to this page as often as is necessary, to become familiar with the sequence.

NOTES

Rests - Silent Beats

Teaching Suggestions:

Concepts:

- Rhythm: Rests (Silent Beats)

If the practice of maintaining a steady beat is well established, the concept of silent beats will not be difficult to master.

Directions:

- Show the students the rests that correspond with the notes with which they are already familiar.

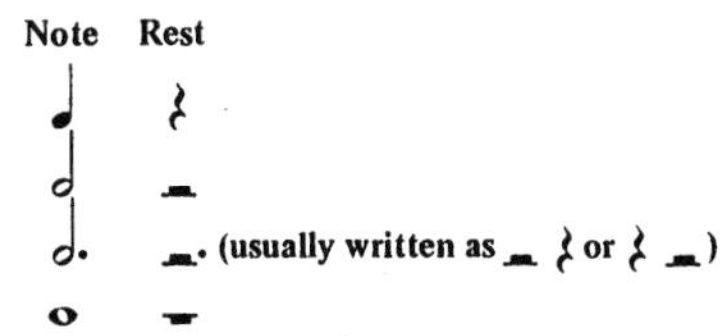

- When counting rests, some teachers prefer to give the rest a quiet sound such as "sh." Other teachers prefer that the rests have no sound at all, and that a physical motion be used to mark the rest. For example:

  1. Tap the forefinger on the lips.

  2. Maintain the motion used to mark the steady beat and "think" the rest.

  3. Move the hands outward like a shrug.

- Read each line on rhythm syllables.

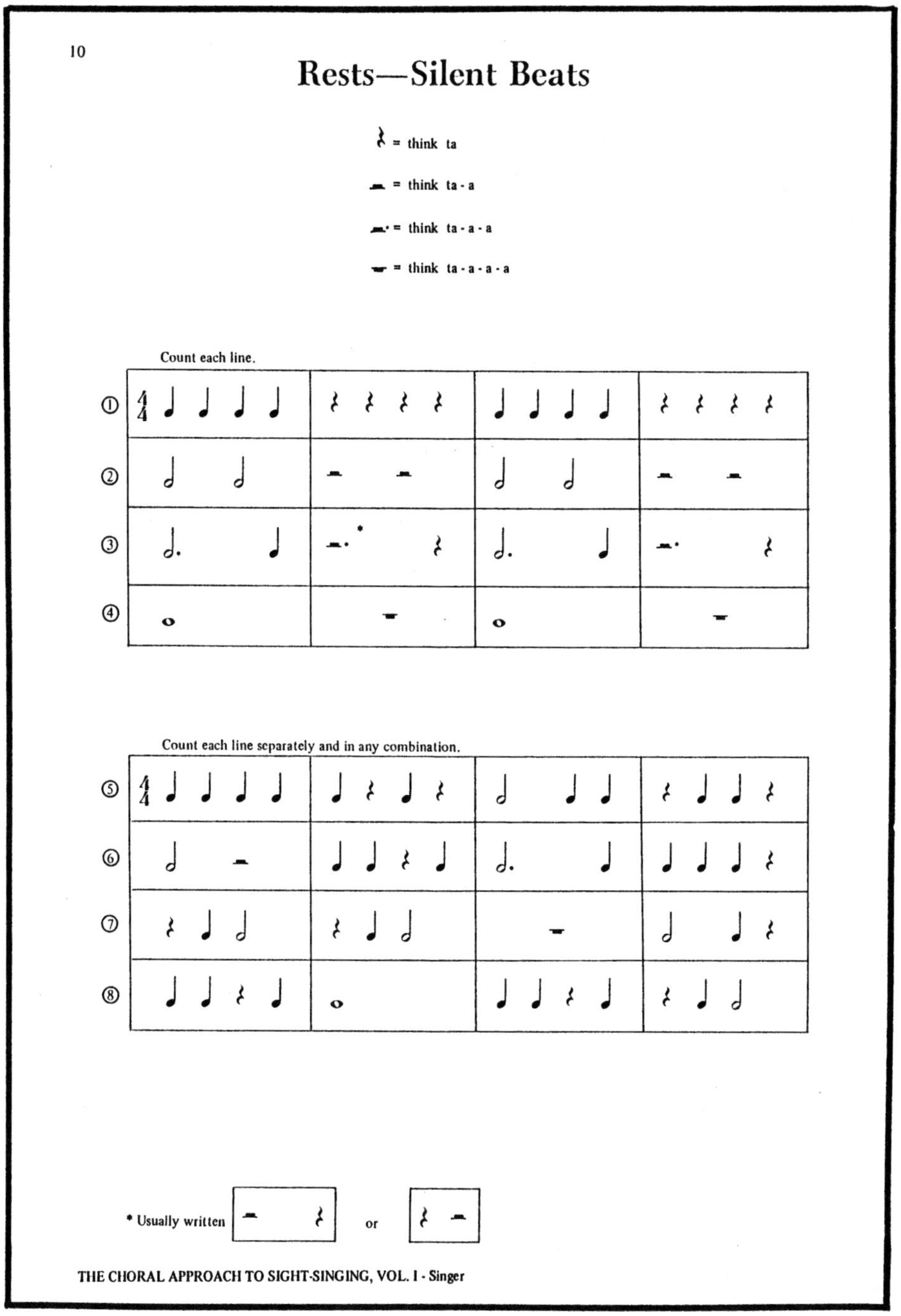
10

Rests—Silent Beats

= think ta
= think ta - a
= think ta - a - a
= think ta - a - a - a

Count each line.

Count each line separately and in any combination.

* Usually written or

THE CHORAL APPROACH TO SIGHT-SINGING, VOL. I - Singer

11

Rests—Singing Exercise III

Sing the exercises in unison or in any combination, using solfege and/or letter names (see page 3).

Higher Voices

①

②

③

Lower Voices

①

②

③

New Notes

High Voices

do re mi fa sol fa mi re do ti la sol la ti do

Low Voices

do re mi fa sol fa mi re do do

THE CHORAL APPROACH TO SIGHT-SINGING, VOL. I - Singer

Singing Exercise III

Teaching Suggestions:

Concepts:

- Rhythm: Rests
- Pitch:

  1. Remembering the pitch after a rest.

  2. New notes for the high voices:

- Harmony: Lines 1, 2, and 3 may be combined to produce harmony.

Directions:

- Lines 1, 2, and 3 are written in both treble and bass clef.
- Say the rhythm.
- Say the pitch syllables (solfege) in rhythm.
- Establish the starting pitch and sing each exercise in solfege.
- The lines may be combined to produce harmony.

NOTE: For variety, have the students switch clefs or sing using letter names, or sing all three lines without stopping. Vary dynamics, tempo, and articulation.

NEW NOTES: This exercise introduces the notes below do for the high voices.

Singing Exercise IV

Teaching Suggestions:

Concepts:

- Rhythm: Rests
- Pitch: Remembering the pitch after a rest.

  Practice new notes for the higher voices.

- Finding the starting pitch when the exercise begins with a rest.

Directions:

- Count each line on rhythm syllables.
- Say the pitch syllables in rhythm.
- Establish the starting pitch and sing each line in solfege.
- Sing the exercises separately and in any combination.
- Try a "follow the leader" game in which the teacher starts singing an exercise and the students must locate, identify, and join in.
- Try some tempo and dynamic variations.

NOTE: For variety, have the girls sing the boys lines and vice versa (in their own register) to reinforce clef relationships.

12

Singing Exercise IV

Sing each exercise in unison or in any combination.

Higher Voices

① ② ③ ④

Lower Voices

⑤ ⑥

THE CHORAL APPROACH TO SIGHT-SINGING, VOL. I - Singer

13

Three Parts Together

The exercises on page 12 are combined here as 3-part songs. Can you follow your own part until it stops at the double bar?

Three To Make Ready

Three To Go

THE CHORAL APPROACH TO SIGHT-SINGING, VOL. I - Singer

Three Parts Together

Teaching Suggestions:

Concepts:

The exercises on this page are exactly the same as those on the previous page, except that three parts are bracketed together into one system.

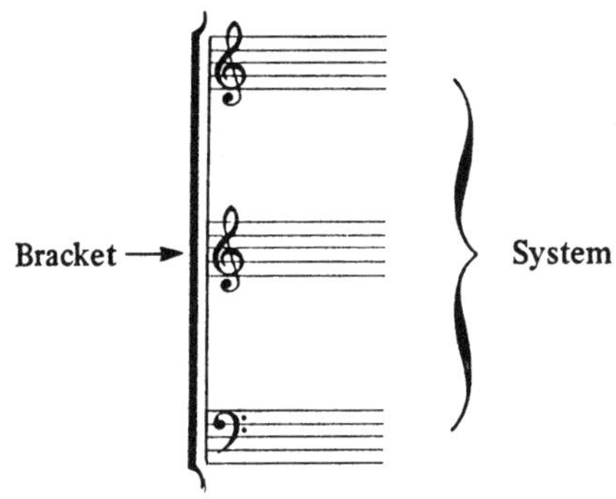

Students should become familiar with the concept of following their own part throughout the music as it moves from one system to the next.

Directions:

- Compare and discuss p. 12 and 13 thoroughly before starting to sing. Point out the brackets and discuss their function.
- Since the singers have already prepared and sight-read the music, it is not necessary to repeat those steps.
- It may be necessary to have the singers point to the line they are singing, as much for the teacher's benefit as for their own, until it is obvious that they understand the purpose of the bracket, and know how to move from one system to the next.

"Oh My! What A Morning"

Teaching Suggestions:

Concepts:

- Rhythm: Rests
- 3-Part song with parts connected by brackets.
- Parts I and II are usually in unison, and Part III is also usually in unison, with some "echo" sections. At the end, the song divides into three-part harmony.

  (Note: The "echo" effect strongly reinforces the function of rests.)
- Repeat sign

Directions:

- Say the rhythm, being careful to leave the correct silences for rests.
- Be sure to discuss and observe the repeat signs.
- Say the pitch syllables in rhythm.
- Establish the pitch and sing the lines separately in solfege. (Each part should sing silently while another is singing aloud.)
- Sing parts together in solfege.
- Sing the song with the text.
- Add the accompaniment.
- Caution against rushing on the final four measures.
- Encourage the students to compare their part to the other parts as they sing.

NOTE: Beware of flatting on "mi" and "ti" anytime, but especially on the last note (Part I) when they must hold a "mi" for 4 beats at the end of their breath.

14

Oh My, What A Morning!

THE CHORAL APPROACH TO SIGHT-SINGING, VOL. I - Singer

15

THE CHORAL APPROACH TO SIGHT-SINGING, VOL. I - Singer

NOTES

The Pitch Ladder (Tonic Chord)

Teaching Suggestions:

Concepts:

- Pitch: The tonic chord

- Establishing the starting pitch

Directions:

- Practice the tonic chord. Changing voices may omit the low D (in parentheses) if it is out of range.
- Sight read "Climb The Hill" following the established sequence.
- Practice establishing the starting pitch for <u>do</u>, <u>mi</u>, or <u>sol</u>.
- Assign a different pitch to different groups and practice building a chord.
- Emphasize the importance of good breathing and posture in producing a good vocal sound.

16

The Pitch Ladder
(Tonic chord)

The notes <u>do</u>, <u>mi</u>, and <u>sol</u>, when sung simultaneously or consecutively produce the tonic chord. Since most songs start on <u>do</u>, <u>mi</u>, or <u>sol</u>, you can use these pitches as a "pitch ladder" to help you find your starting pitch.

Climb The Hill

Sing a pitch ladder and then sing this exercise in solfege.

To find your starting pitch, sing the complete pitch ladder, then climb to the starting pitch for your part. Some of the exercises on the following page start on notes other than <u>do</u>.

THE CHORAL APPROACH TO SIGHT-SINGING, VOL. I - Singer

17

Pitch Ladder Practice

Sing these two-line exercises in unison and in any combination.

THE CHORAL APPROACH TO SIGHT-SINGING, VOL. I - Singer

Pitch Ladder Practice

Teaching Suggestions:

Concepts:

- Interval skips within the tonic chord

Directions:

- For all lines, speak the rhythm first, speak pitch syllables in rhythm, establish the starting pitch with a tonic chord, sing the exercises in unison.
- Encourage the high voices and low voices to read the other's part.
- Combine lines to produce harmony.
- For variety, experiment with different dynamics, tempos, and articulations, for example: sing a line normally and then add an accellerando or ritardando.

"Let Your Voice Be Heard"

Teaching Suggestions:

Concepts:

- Starting a song in harmony
- Skips within the tonic chord
- Alike and different phrases
- Homophonic texture (all parts have the same rhythm)
- Other "Majestically" (see "style word")
  f (forte)

Directions:

- Read the rhythm.
- Read pitch syllables in rhythm.
- Find phrases which are alike. Find phrases which are similar. Determine form (Intro A A' B B A)
- Isolate interval skips, parts separately and parts together, especially measures 8-9 where the chord moves from 1st to 2nd inversion in the vocal parts. Practice this carefully, listening for balance, tuning, and blend.
- Establish the starting pitch and sing a cappella on pitch syllables. Repeat, if necessary, allowing the singers to correct their own mistakes. After twice through if they are still making errors, isolate and correct.
- Sing with accompaniment on pitch syllables.
- Sing with text, a cappella.
- Sing complete, with text and accompaniment.

19
Let it ring o'er all the
Let it ring o'er all the
Let it ring o'er all the
13
earth. Let all na - tions hear our
earth. Let all na - tions hear our
earth. Let all na - tions hear our
13
THE CHORAL APPROACH TO SIGHT-SINGING, VOL. I - Singer

NOTES

NOTES

20
joy - ous sound, and spread the news the world a - round. Oh
joy - ous sound, and spread the news the world a - round. Oh
joy - ous sound, and spread the news the world a - round. Oh
17
let your voice be heard.
let your voice be heard.
let your voice be heard.
17
THE CHORAL APPROACH TO SIGHT-SINGING, VOL. I - Singer

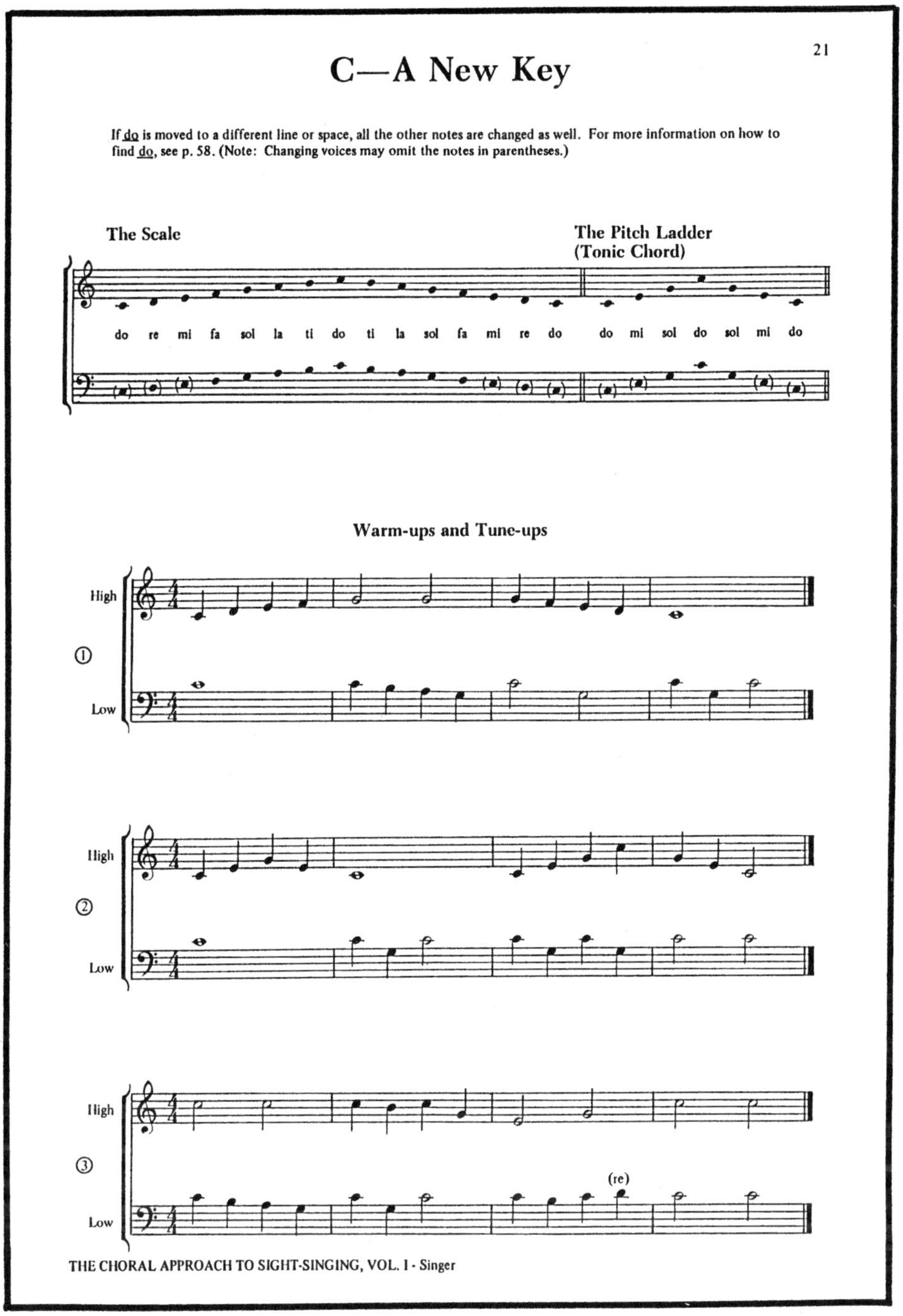
21

C—A New Key

If do is moved to a different line or space, all the other notes are changed as well. For more information on how to find do, see p. 58. (Note: Changing voices may omit the notes in parentheses.)

THE CHORAL APPROACH TO SIGHT-SINGING, VOL. I - Singer

C - A New Key

Teaching Suggestions:

Concepts:

- A new key - C
- Pitch ladder (tonic chord) in the key of C
- Optional notes for changed voices
- 2-Part systems with parts I and II in unison

Directions:

- Read the directions at the top of the page in the student book. A helpful analogy might be that of a "family" moving, where relationships stay the same, only the location is different.
- Sing the scale, letting the lower voices experience the optional notes, if possible. Do this several times to get used to the "feel" of the new key.
- Prepare and sing Exercise 1, using previously established procedures.
- Sing the pitch ladder several times, using the notes in parentheses if possible.
- Prepare and sing Exercises 2 and 3.

NOTE: Point out the high "re" in the boys part. From time to time, new elements of music will be introduced in this manner (without a lot of explanation). The function will in all cases be obvious.

Key Of C Exercises

Teaching Suggestions:

Concepts:

- Key of C Practice
- Pick-up notes

Directions:

- Prepare and sight read each line using previously established procedures.
- Pick-up Notes: If you are using the Kodaly system of rhythm syllables, the concept of an incomplete measure will be quite simple. "Ta" is "ta" no matter where it occurs. You may wish to emphasize the concept of meter at this point, i.e., the first beat of a measure receives a stronger stress. If you are using another counting system, such as numbers, demonstrate pick-up notes this way:

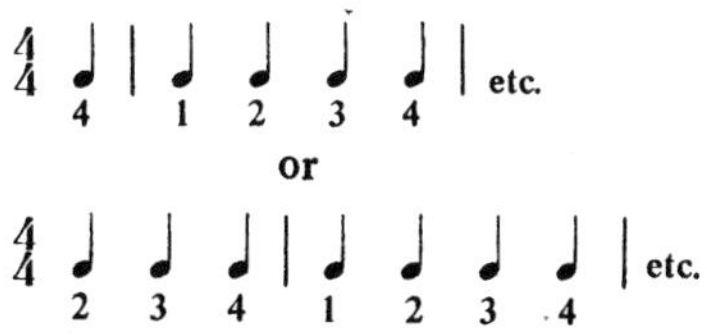

NOTE: In keeping with current music editing practice, in a piece with a pick-up note, the last bar is a complete bar. You may wish to look for examples of older music where this is not the case.

For fully changed voices, middle C may seem to be high in the range. To help establish the starting pitch, start on G and sing up the scale:

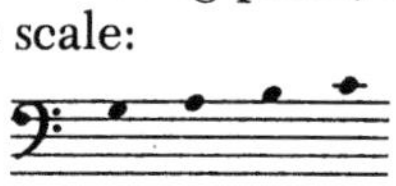

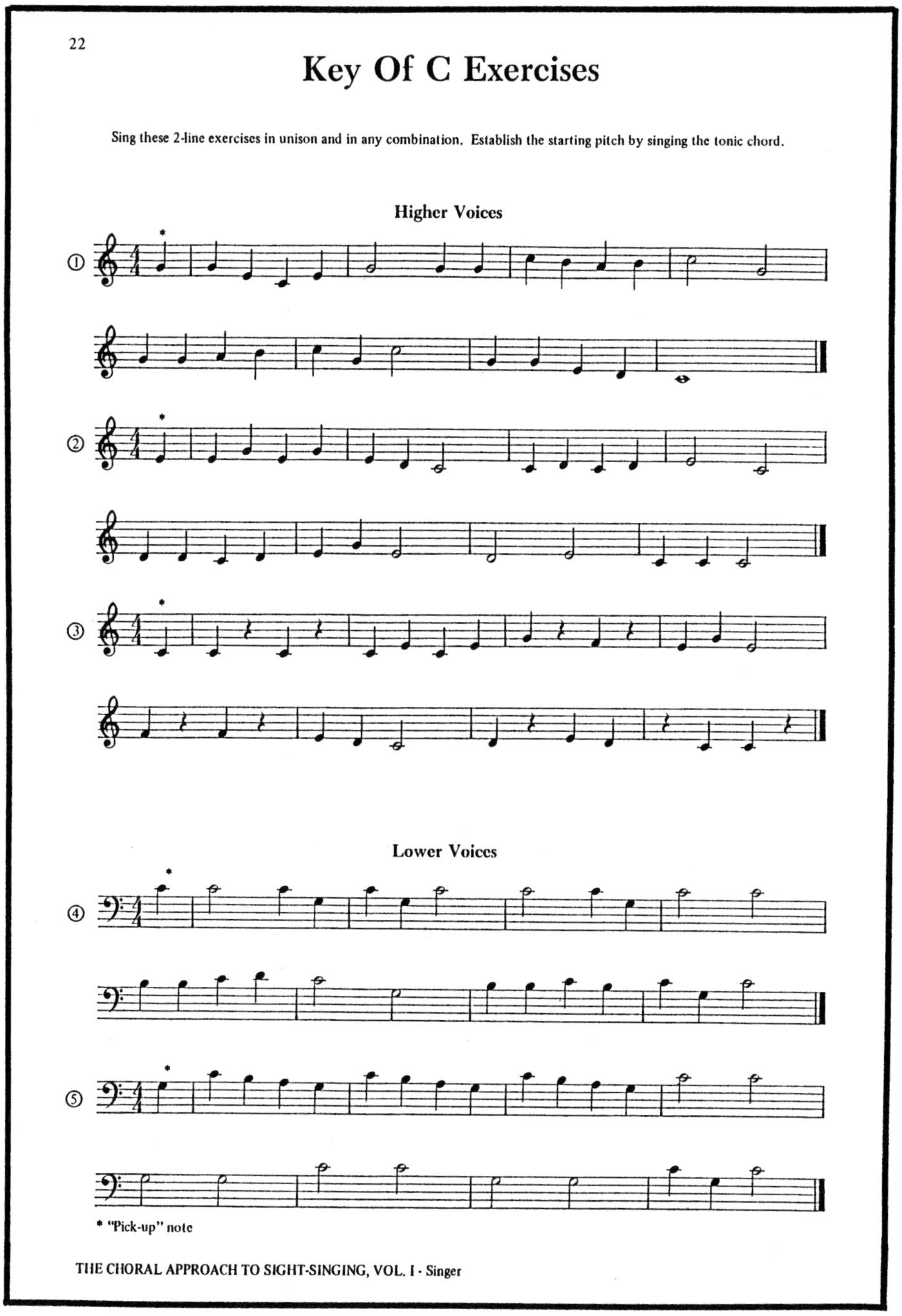

Also practice with the changed voices in falsetto, starting on a third space C and vocalizing downward on "ooh", keeping the lips small and rounded, with lots of breath support. Although their voices may break at first, with practice and maturity, they will eventually be able to sing in this mid-range without difficulty.

New Patterns

Teaching Suggestions:

Concepts:

- Eighth notes (two sounds on a beat)

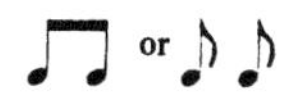

Directions:

- Establish the steady beat and demonstrate eighth notes using the "ti" for each eighth note:

  Point out that where the quarter note gets the beat, eighth notes are two sounds on one beat.

  Repeat this exercise, this time with the students.

- Read each line of the rhythm exercise on rhythm syllables. (Variations: Read in canon or combine lines; make up new combinations)

3-Part Practice

- Read each part in rhythm, finding the place where Part III has a different rhythm. Read again with parts together.
- Read parts separately on pitch syllables in rhythm. (NOTE: When one part reads aloud, the other parts should read silently.) Combine parts.
- Sing a tonic chord to establish the starting pitch and sight-read parts together, keeping a steady beat throughout.

The Fox And The Grapes

Teaching Suggestions:

Concepts:

Pitch:
- Key of C
- Skips within the tonic chord

Rhythm:
- Eighth notes

Other:
- Repeat sign
- First and second endings

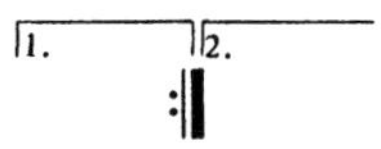

Directions:

- Have the students determine whether all parts have the same rhythm (homophonic). Read the song on rhythm syllables, keeping a steady beat.
- Read the song on pitch syllables (or letter names) in rhythm. (While one part reads aloud the other parts practice silently.) Read the song parts together on pitch syllables in rhythm. Find the place where the parts are in unison.
- Sing a tonic chord to establish the pitch and sing the song on pitch syllables. Repeat, allowing the students to correct their own mistakes. If errors remain, isolate those spots and correct them. (NOTE: Beats 3 and 4 of the first ending may be especially tricky.)
- Sing the song with text. Allow the students to determine the dynamics.

Eighth Note Practice

Teaching Suggestions:

Concepts:

Pitch:
- Key of C
- Skips within the tonic chord
- Range of a full octave for the higher voices
- Lower voice range of sol-re
- Finding the starting pitch with the tonic chord

Rhythm:
- Eighth notes
- Review of all other rhythms studied, and reinforcement of the steady beat

Other:
- Interesting dissonances occur in some of the combinable lines. This will help the singers to become aware of parts other than their own.

Directions:

- Prepare and sight-read each line using previously established procedures.
- Before you try to combine the lines, do a spot check comparison, so you can determine the best possible tempo.
- Start slowly at first, but try a faster tempo after the singers become more confident.
- Sing the exercises separately at first, and then in any combination.

Short Songs - Key Of C

Teaching Suggestions:

Concepts:

- Each line is affected by what is happening in other lines.
- Rests
- Key of C
- Eighth notes

Directions:

"Follow"

- Be brave and try a different approach to this exercise.
- Count the rhythm of each line.
- Establish the starting pitch of all three parts.
- Try to sight-read all three parts simultaneously in solfege.
- Repeat, maybe twice, to see if the singers can correct their own mistakes. If not, isolate and correct.
- Sing again with the text.

"Name That Tune" ("Camptown Races" or "Doo-Dah")

- Count the rhythm of Part I. Any guesses?
- Sing Part I in solfege. Any guesses?
- Prepare the other parts using previously established procedures.
- Can anyone remember the words?
- Watch out for the extra "ti" in Part II.

Three Bluebirds

Teaching Suggestions:

Pitch:
- Key of C
- Skips within the tonic chord

Rhythm:
- Eighth notes

Form:
- Alike/different
- Sequence

Other:

- *f* forte
- staccato (in piano)
- Part III "solo" section

Directions:

- Find the spot where Part III has a special featured section and parts I and II have rests.
- Read the song parts together on rhythm syllables.
- Find the lines which are alike or almost alike. Find the section which has a melodic pattern which repeats each time at a higher pitch. (Sequence - measure 4-6, parts I and II) Find where the parts are in unison.
- Sing a tonic chord to establish the pitch and sight-read on pitch syllables. Repeat, allowing singers to correct their own mistakes. If any errors remain, isolate and correct.
- Repeat with accompaniment.
- Sing a cappella with text.
- Sing accompanied with text.

NOTES

28
sat up - on a wall all on a sum - mer morn - ing.
sat up - on a wall all on a sum - mer morn - ing.
sat up - on a wall all on a sum - mer morn - ing. The
11
Flew off the wall, flew off the wall.
Flew off the wall, flew off the wall.
first one, he flew off the wall, flew off the wall, flew off the wall. The
11
THE CHORAL APPROACH TO SIGHT-SINGING, VOL. I - Singer

29
all on a sum - mer
all on a sum - mer
sec - ond one he flew off the wall all on a sum - mer
19
morn - ing. The third one he was - n't there at all so
morn - ing. The third one he was - n't there at all so
morn - ing. The third one he was - n't there at all so
19
THE CHORAL APPROACH TO SIGHT-SINGING, VOL. I - Singer

NOTES

NOTES

30
noth - ing's left up - on the wall. No blue - birds
noth - ing's left up - on the wall. No blue - birds
noth - ing's left up - on the wall. No blue - birds
sit - ting on a wall all - on a sum - mer morn - ing.
sit - ting on a wall all on a sum - mer morn - ing.
sit - ting on a wall all on a sum - mer morn - ing.
THE CHORAL APPROACH TO SIGHT-SINGING, VOL. I - Singer

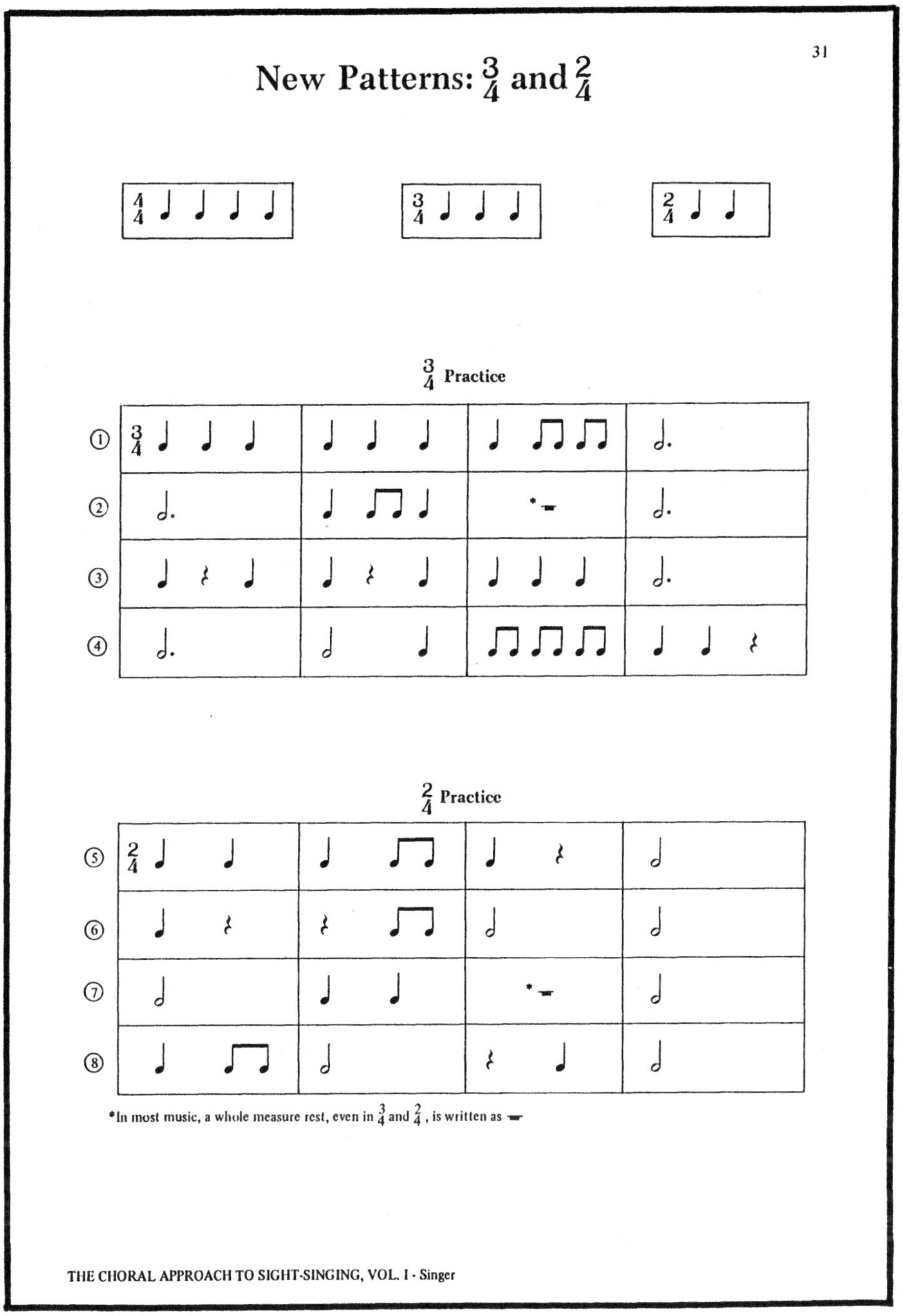

New Patterns - $\frac{3}{4}$ and $\frac{2}{4}$

Teaching Suggestions:

Concepts:

$\frac{3}{4}$ - 3 beats in a measure

$\frac{2}{4}$ - 2 beats in a measure

Directions:

- Point out that 3 over 4 and 2 over 4 are not really fractions, but rather are indications of how many beats there are in a measure (the top number) and what kind of note gets the beat (the bottom number).
- Say the rhythm of each exercise.
- Be sure to keep the rhythm steady, especially on the rests.

NOTE: Meter signature concepts are musically self-explanatory in this method. Depending on the maturity of the group, you may wish to keep explanations at a minimum.

$\frac{3}{4}$ and $\frac{2}{4}$ Practice
(Key of G)

Teaching Suggestions:

Concepts:

- $\frac{3}{4}$ and $\frac{2}{4}$ meter (The quarter note "ta" remains constant no matter what the meter is, $\frac{2}{4}$, $\frac{3}{4}$, or $\frac{4}{4}$
- Key of G (for a review, turn back to page 5)
- Introduction of single eighth notes and rests

Directions:

- Review the key of G as needed (See page 5)
- Count exercises 1-6. More than likely, there will be no problems.
- Prepare and sight-read each line using previously established procedures.
- Sing lines 1-6 separately and in any combination.
- Prepare the $\frac{3}{4}$ exercises $\frac{2}{4}$ the same way. (Remember, you cannot combine the $\frac{3}{4}$ and $\frac{2}{4}$ lines!)
- Exercises 9, 10, and 12 all use single eighth notes and eighth rests. Demonstrate the way these rhythms are counted and practice until the students can perform them accurately.

NOTE: This is a good page to review often for warm-ups, tone blending, and note/rest precision. Even when the students have mastered it completely, it will sharpen awareness of rhythmic precision and good pitch.

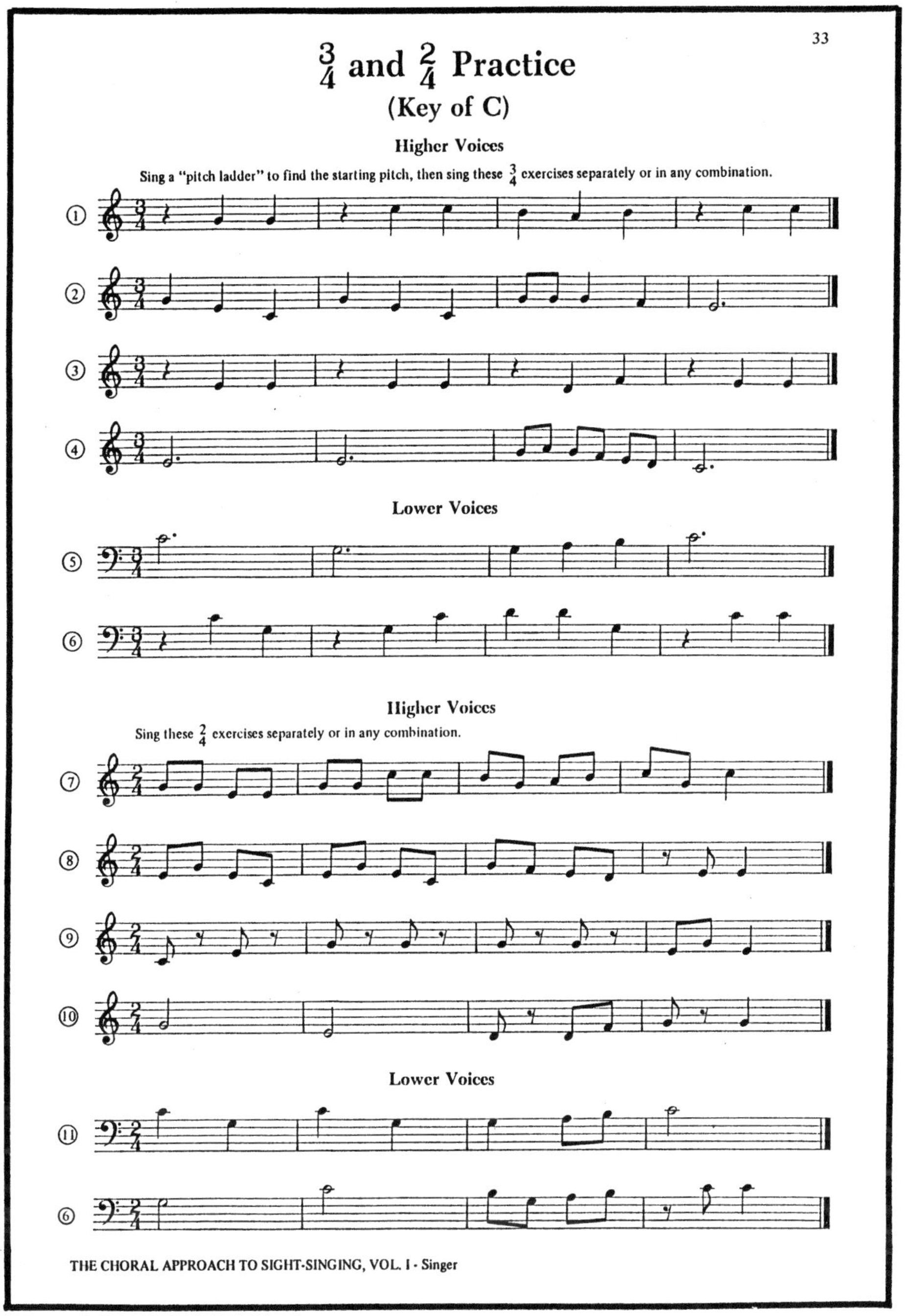

$\frac{3}{4}$ and $\frac{2}{4}$ Practice
(Key Of C)

Teaching Suggestions:

Concepts:

- Sharpen note reading skills by changing keys and meters
- Reinforce previously introduced rhythm patterns

Directions:

- Prepare and sight-read each line using previously established procedures.
- Sight-read the $\frac{3}{4}$ lines (1-6) separately and in any combinations.
- Sight-read the $\frac{2}{4}$ lines (7-12) separately and in any combination.
- Keep the tempo steady, don't rush!
- Stress the importance of the rests.

NOTE: Encourage the character of 3/4 and 2/4. Which sounds like "oom-pah-pah" and which sounds more like a march? What other descriptions come to mind?

"Old Joe Atkinson"

Teaching Suggestions:

Concepts:

- Reinforce $\frac{2}{4}$
- Reinforce key of C
- Melodic and rhythmic fragments that are alike or very similar

Directions:

- Prepare and sight-read each line using previously established procedures. (Singers should read silently while another part is reading aloud.) Or, count the rhythm, establish the pitch and attempt all three lines simultaneously on solfege syllables.
- Give them another chance or two to try this alternate method.
- Add the words, which really give variety, especially to a somewhat dull Part II.
- Encourage them to "give a good try" on projects like this, whether in this book or in other materials. Be sure to compliment the parts they get right, rather than dwell on the sections they missed. Always give them a chance to correct their own mistakes before you jump in to rescue them. They have to have the freedom to fail and "dig themselves out." It's a vital part of the learning process.

"Characters"

Teaching Suggestions:

Concepts:

- Reinforce $\frac{3}{4}$ and key of G
- Repeat sign, 1st and 2nd endings
- A longer song with two verses, requiring a longer span of concentration
- Pick-up note in the 1st ending
- "Preview" of tied notes in the 2nd ending

Directions:

- Prepare and sight-read using previously established procedures. (Singers read silently while another part reads aloud.)
- Sing the song parts together in solfege.
- Add the words.
- Review as needed, making sure the lines are sung musically, with critical attention to good pitch, specifically "mi" and "ti" and especially on cadences.
- If there are questions about the tied note in the second ending, you may wish to jump ahead to page 38. Briefly, to count tied notes, eliminate the consonant "t" on the second note of the tie.

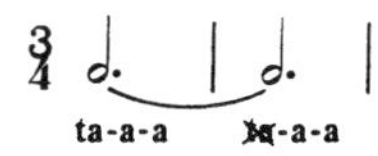

Warm-ups And Tune-ups
Key of G

Concepts:

Pitch:
- Introduce skips within the dominant and sub-dominant chords.

Harmony:
- Introduce chord drills as a device for developing a vertical concept of harmony (how each part relates to the whole) and as a technique for refining balance, tuning, and blend.
- The addition of an optional 4th (bass) part.

Directions:

NOTE: Take this page in small doses!

- Introduce the first exercise on pitch syllables, parts separately, and practice several times to become familiar with the new intervals of the dominant and sub-dominant chords.
- Sing parts together, listening carefully for balance, tuning, and blend.

Chord Drills

- Introduce the chord drills to the choir, adding the optional bass part, if there are enough low voices in the choir.
- Build the first chord of each example from the bottom up, or the top down. The director should dictate each chord. Singers should use staggered breathing and should listen carefully for balance, tuning, and blend.
- Experiment with dynamics, using crescendo and decrescendo. Sing the examples on different neutral syllables (loo, lo, la, etc.). Sing Drill 6 on the syllables "mee, meh, mah, moh, moo"

NOTE: Return to this page often, especially before sight-reading or rehearsing a song in G major.

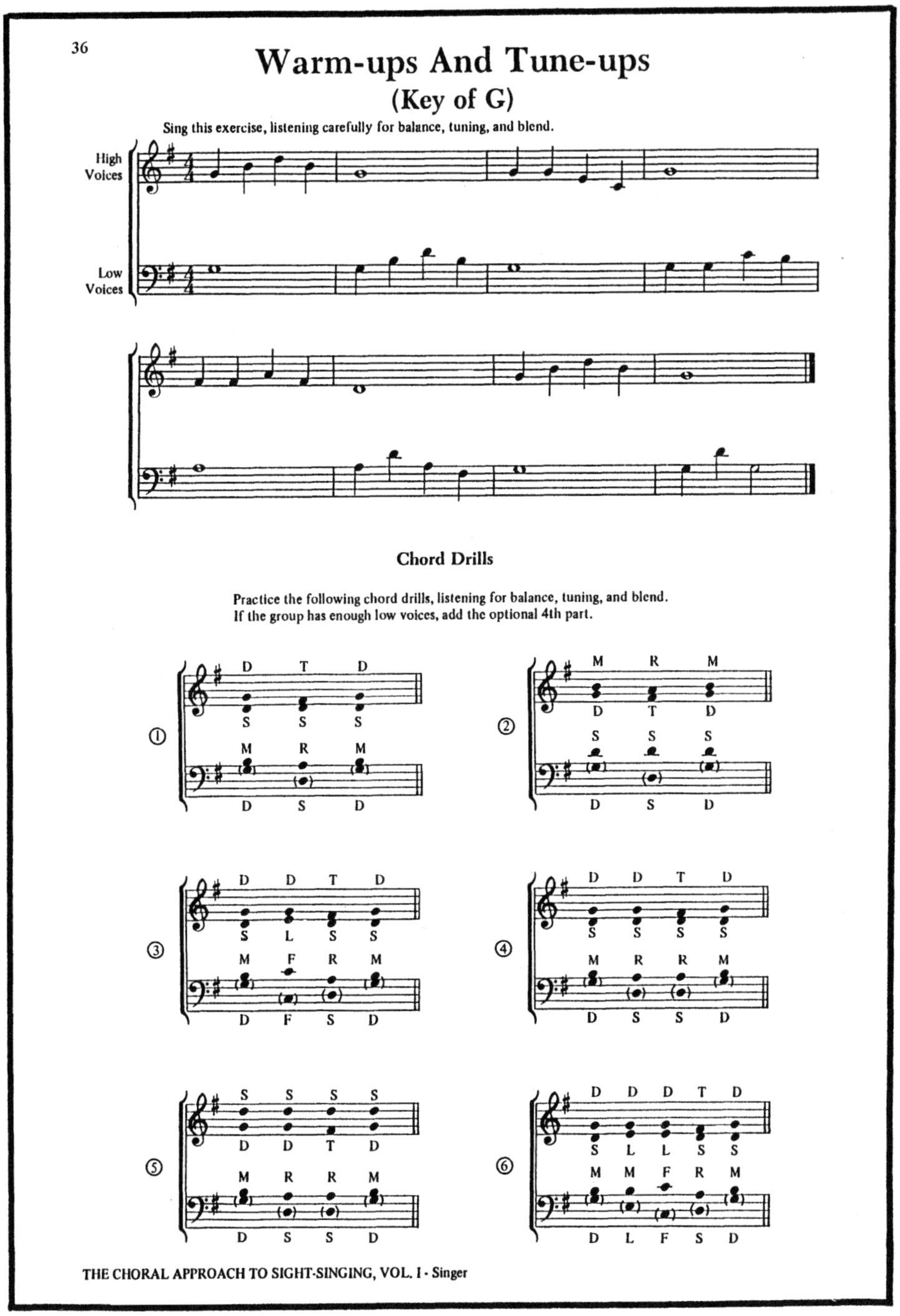
36

Warm-ups And Tune-ups
(Key of G)

Sing this exercise, listening carefully for balance, tuning, and blend.

Chord Drills

Practice the following chord drills, listening for balance, tuning, and blend.
If the group has enough low voices, add the optional 4th part.

THE CHORAL APPROACH TO SIGHT-SINGING, VOL. I - Singer

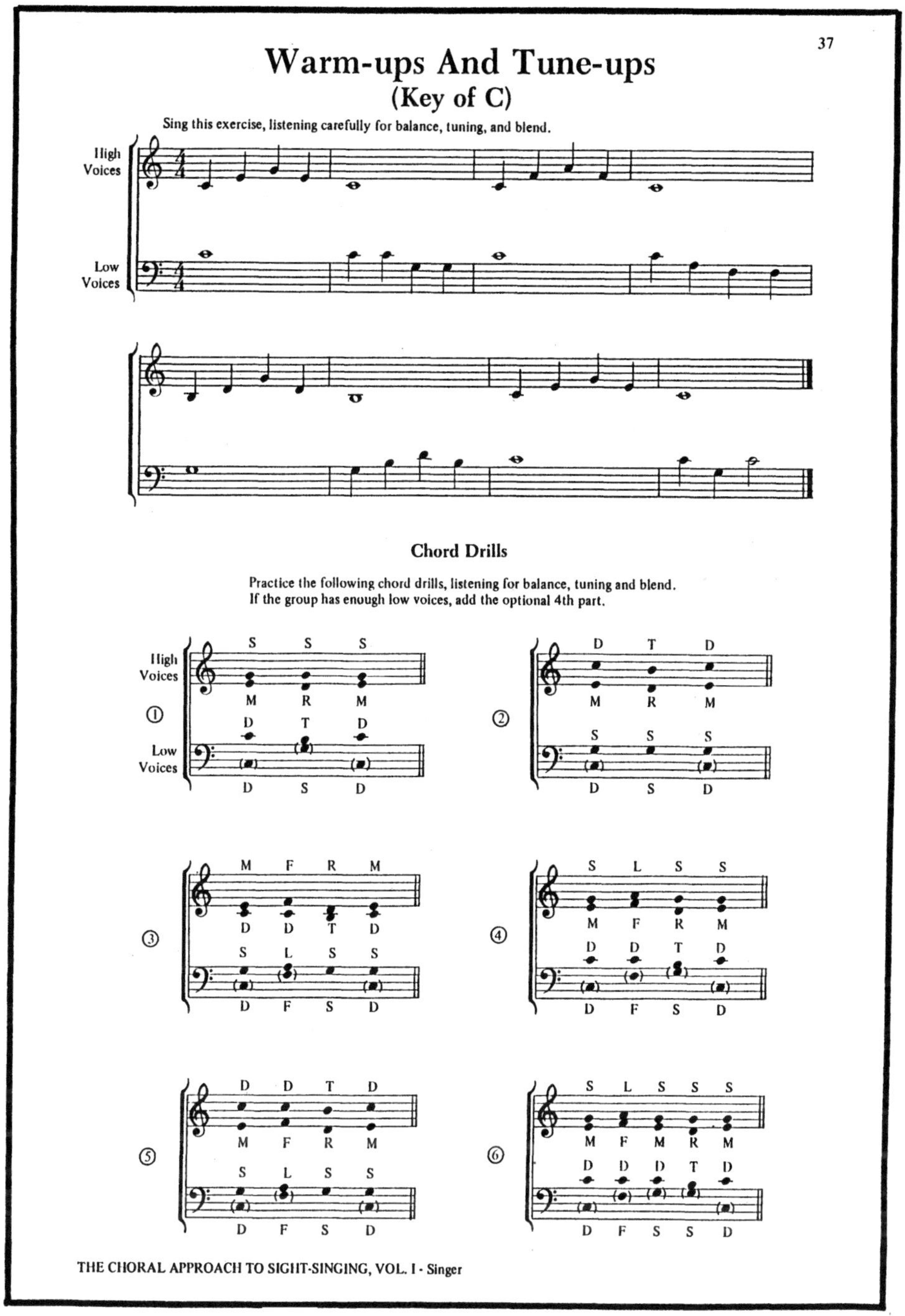

Warm-ups And Tune-ups

Key of C

Concepts and directions for this page are the same as those on page 38. For similar exercises and chord drills in other keys, see page 59 and following.

Ties

Teaching Suggestions:

NOTE: The next few pages provide the students with somewhat more challenging rhythmic concepts to master. Consequently, care has been taken to simplify the melodic demands, so as to allow for greater concentration on the rhythm.

Concepts:

Pitch: Key of G

Rhythm: Tied notes

Directions:

NOTE: Using the neutral syllables "ta" and "ti" make it easier to master the concept of ties than if using the number system of counting.

- Explain to students that a tie "ties" together two notes of the same pitch.
- Refer to the examples and demonstrate how they are counted. Have the students perform the examples.
- Read lines 1-4 on rhythm syllables, repeating until students are secure.
- Read lines 5-6 on rhythm syllables, then on pitch syllables.
- Establish the starting pitch and sing lines 5-6, maintaining a steady beat.
- Repeat, if necessary, allowing students to correct their own mistakes. If any errors remain, isolate and correct.

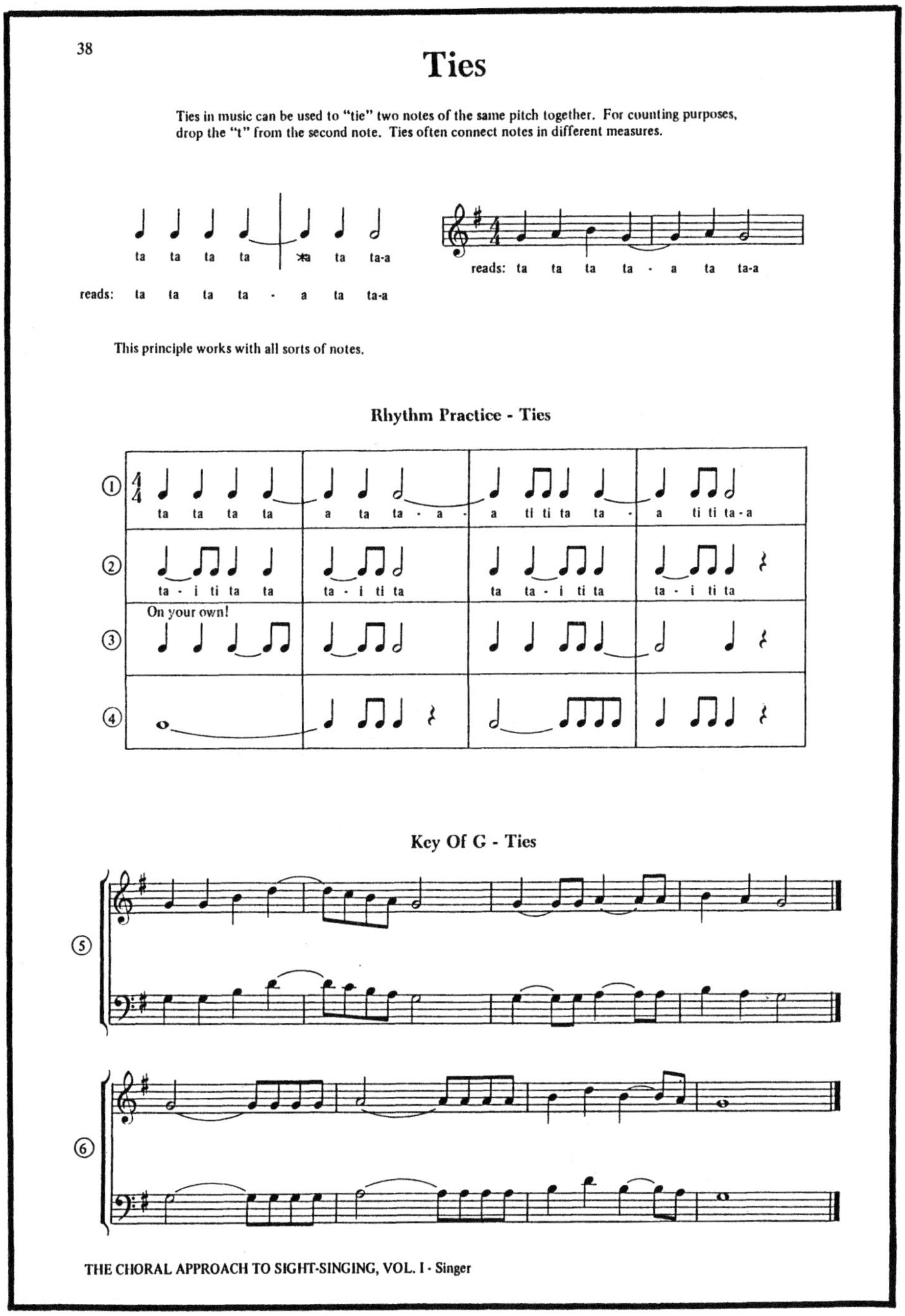

38

Ties

Ties in music can be used to "tie" two notes of the same pitch together. For counting purposes, drop the "t" from the second note. Ties often connect notes in different measures.

This principle works with all sorts of notes.

Rhythm Practice - Ties

Key Of G - Ties

THE CHORAL APPROACH TO SIGHT-SINGING, VOL. I - Singer

More Practice With Ties

Teaching Suggestions:

Concepts:

- Key of G
- Key of C
- Tied notes
- Pick-up notes

Directions:

- Scan over the key of G exercise and find the places that are alike and different.
- Read each part separately on rhythm syllables (the other part reads silently) and then read parts together. Stress the importance of keeping a steady beat throughout.
- Read in rhythm on pitch syllables.
- Establish the starting pitch and sing on pitch syllables. As always, allow the singers to correct their own mistakes, but if errors remain, isolate and correct.

"When The Saints Go Marching In" (Key of C)

- Read parts together on syllables.
- Read in rhythm on pitch syllables.
- Establish the starting pitch, and sing in solfege. Repeat with the text, isolating mistakes and correcting, if needed.

Slurs

Teaching Suggestions:

Concepts:

- Ties connect notes of the same pitch.
- Slurs connect notes of different pitches. In singing, a slur is used when there is more than one note on a single word or syllable.

Directions:

- Read and discuss the explanation of ties and slurs in the student book.
- Read the rhythm of the example, read it in solfege, sing it in solfege, sing it on the text. NOTE: The effect of the slur is not evident until sung with text.

"Clear Sailing"

- Read through silently, noting where the slurs occur.
- Sight-read, using previously established procedures.
- Add the text.

40

Slurs

Be careful not to confuse ties with slurs. Both look the same, but a tie connects two notes of the SAME pitch, while a slur connects two or more notes of a DIFFERENT pitch.

When you count music with slurs, you don't take the "t" sound off the second note.

In singing, a slur is used when you have more than one note on a single word or syllable.

Clear Sailing

THE CHORAL APPROACH TO SIGHT-SINGING, VOL. I - Singer

More Practice With Slurs

Teaching Suggestions:

Concepts:

- Reinforce concept of slurs
- 3-Part Practice in the keys of G and C
- Pick-up notes
- Fermata 𝄐

Directions:

- For both of these short songs, scan through silently noting slurs and other spots that might be difficult.
- Read through on rhythm syllables, then on pitch syllables in rhythm. (Singers should read silently when another part is reading aloud.)
- Establish the starting pitch and sight-read parts together in solfege.
- Repeat as necessary, allowing the singers to correct their own mistakes.
- Sing the song with the text.
- Vary tempo and dynamics.

Dotted Notes

Teaching Suggestions:

Concepts:

- Dotted notes are another way of writing tied notes:

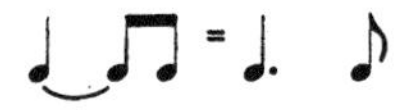

- Both the tied note and the dotted note are made longer by eliminating the "t" consonant.

  NOTE: The reverse pattern:

  may seem awkward until the singers become accustomed to it.

Directions:

- Review the examples in the boxes.
- Sing the two versions of "America" and note the similarities to the examples in the boxes.
- Count the first two lines of "Rhythm Practice"
- Isolate the 1st measure of line 3. Discuss it and demonstrate it, if necessary.
- Count lines 3 and 4.
- Count all four lines without stopping.
- For fun, count the measures "bingo-style." Up, down, angled, backwards? This adds variety to review.
- Make up your own examples.

42

Dotted Notes

Tied notes can be written another way by using a dot to replace the second tied note.

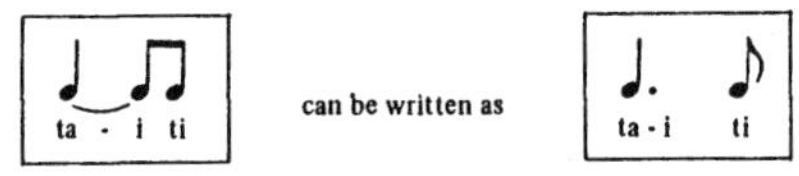

By using dots, a song like this one:

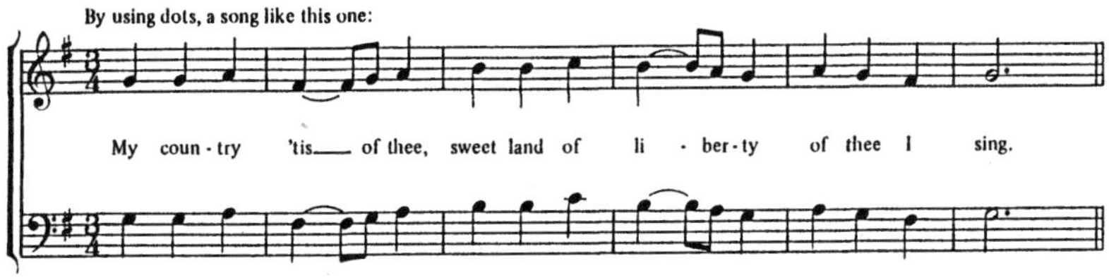

can be written this way:

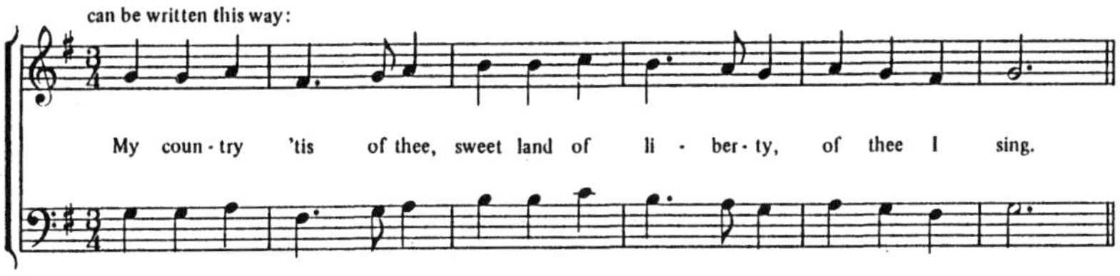

Rhythm Practice

THE CHORAL APPROACH TO SIGHT-SINGING, VOL. I - Singer

Dotted Note Practice

Teaching Suggestions:

Concepts:

- Reinforce dotted notes

- Combinable exercises
- Introduce low "fa" (Exercise 3)
- Review larger intervals

Directions:

- Prepare each line by the usual procedure. Remember to use the tonic chord (pitch ladder) to help establish the starting pitch.
- Try to sing the whole page in solfege, starting from top to bottom. If they can't sing all the notes, have them keep track of where they are and fade in and out as necessary, making allowances for the range, clef, etc. No matter what, keep going! Stress that anyone can get lost, but it is a great skill to be able to find your place and get back in!
- Sing the lines separately and in any combination.
- For variety, change the tempo and dynamics.

"America"

Teaching Suggestions:

Concepts:

- Reinforce

  ♩. ♪

- Reinforce slurs
- Rhythmic and melodic sequences
- Since this is a familiar melody, this song would be a good choice to attempt to sight-read with the text right away.

Directions:

- Be brave! Establish the starting pitches and sight-read the piece complete with words the first time. Since the melody is familiar, the rhythm should not be difficult, and Part I will hold the group together.
- Repeat so that Parts II and III can correct their own errors.
- Note the rhythmic and melodic sequences and encourage them to always look for places that are the same or almost the same.
- Part I and II can switch parts in order to give the sopranos an additional sight-reading experience.

"Hold On!"

Teaching Suggestions:

Concepts:

- Dotted note patterns:

  ♩. ♪ and ♪ ♩.

- Slurs and ties
- Dynamic contrasts
- Phrases which are alike or almost alike (1, 2, 4)
- Looking ahead to anticipate problems (finding the pitch: last note of measure 8 to the first note of measure 9)

Directions:

- Encourage the students to find the sections which are alike or almost alike (phrases 1, 2, and 4).
- Before sight-reading, isolate the last note of measure 8 to the first note of the measure 9. Practice this a few times until it is secure.
- Isolate the last note of the bridge section (m. 12) and practice going into m. 13.
- Count the rhythm.
- Depending on the maturity of the group, you may be able to skip the usual steps and sight-read right away on the words.
- Try again and let the singers correct their own errors.

"Swing Low, Sweet Chariot"

Teaching Suggestions:

Concepts:

- Dotted rhythms:

  ♩. ♪ and ♪ ♩.
- Slurs, ties
- Key of G
- High "la" (Part I) and low "mi" (Part II)
- Skips within the tonic and subdominant chords
- Augmentation (M. 25-28)

Directions:

- Say the rhythm using rhythm syllables, noting the places where the parts have the same rhythm (homophonic).
- Say the pitch syllables in rhythm together or parts separately.
- Establish the starting pitch and sing through a cappella in solfege.
- Repeat, if necessary, allowing the singers to correct their own mistakes.
- Add the text.
- Add the accompaniment.
- Encourage the students to find the section which is just like another section, but the rhythms are twice as long (augmentation-M. 25-28).

47
char - i - ot, coming for to car - ry me home.
char - i - ot, coming for to car - ry me, car - ry me home.
char - i - ot, coming for to car - ry me home. I
11
Oh, what did I see coming for to car - ry me home? A
Oh, what did I see coming for to car - ry me home?
looked o - ver Jor - dan coming for to car - ry me home?
11
THE CHORAL APPROACH TO SIGHT-SINGING, VOL. I - Singer

NOTES

NOTES

48
band of an - gels com-ing af - ter me, com-ing for to car - ry me
Oh, com-ing af - ter me, com-ing for to car - ry me,
Oh, com-ing af - ter me, com-ing for to car - ry me
19
home. Swing low, sweet char - i - ot, com-ing for to car - ry me
car - ry me home. Swing low, sweet char - i - ot, com-ing for to car - ry me
home. Swing low, sweet char - i - ot, com-ing for to car - ry me
19
THE CHORAL APPROACH TO SIGHT-SINGING, VOL. I - Singer

49
home. Swing low, sweet char - i - ot,
home. Swing low, sweet char - i - ot,
home. Swing low, sweet char - i - ot,
com - ing for to car - ry me home.
com - ing for to car - ry me, car - ry me home.
com - ing for to car - ry me home.
THE CHORAL APPROACH TO SIGHT-SINGING, VOL. I - Singer

NOTES

F - A New Key

Teaching Suggestions:

Concepts:

- Pitch: Key of F Scale and tonic chord
- Optional notes for changed voices

Directions:

- Sing the scale and tonic chord in the new key several times to become familiar with do's new locations.
- Prepare and sing each exercise, using previously established procedures.

50

F—A New Key

The next few pages feature exercises and songs in the key of F. Sing the scale and the tonic chord to become familiar with do's new location. (Note: Changing voices may omit the notes in parentheses.)

THE CHORAL APPROACH TO SIGHT-SINGING, VOL. I - Singer

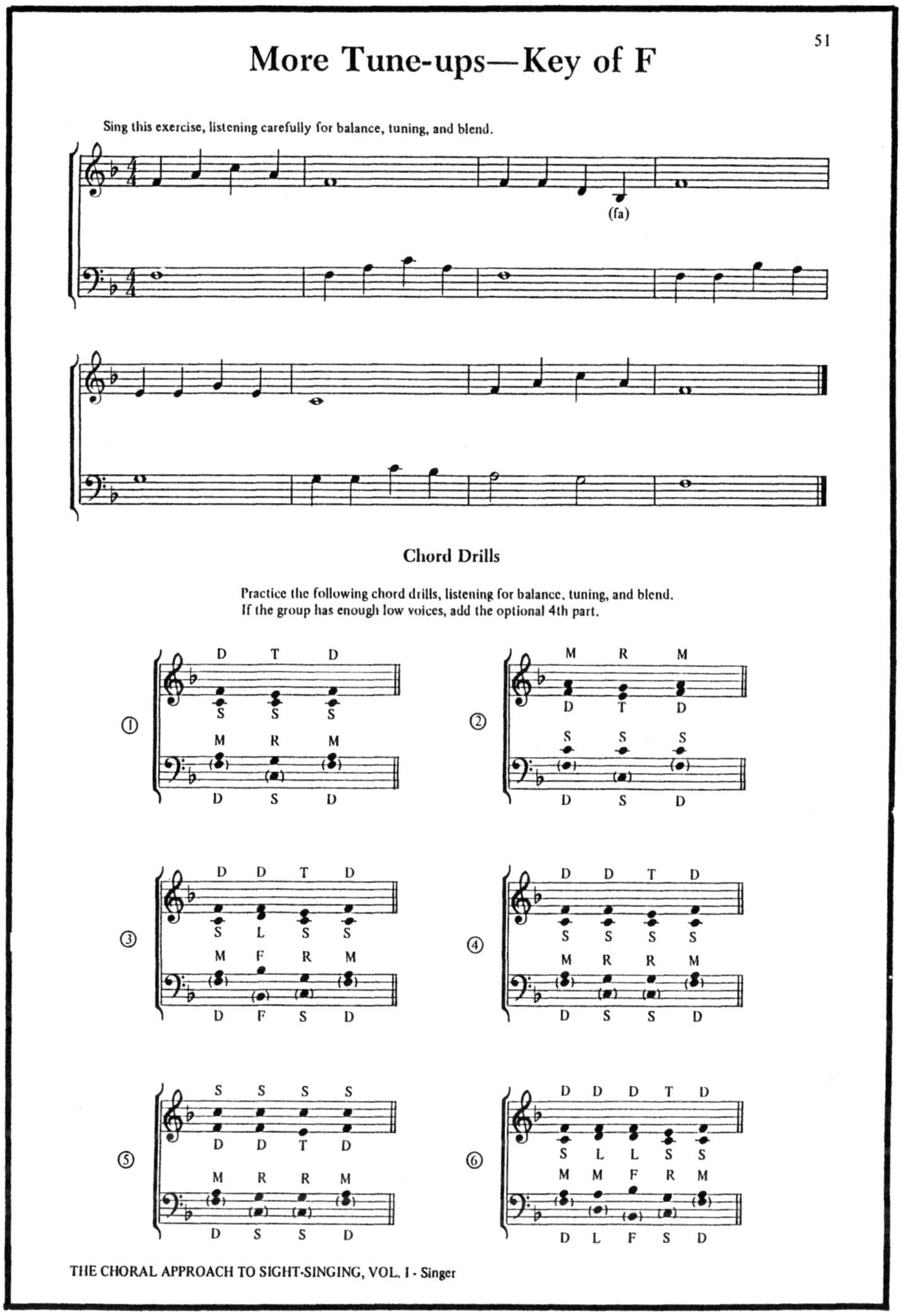

More Tune-Ups - Key of F

Teaching Suggestions:

Concepts:

- Key of F
- Skips in the tonic, dominant, and sub-dominant chords (including low "fa" for treble voices)
- Chord progressions including an optional 4th (bass) part

Directions:

- Sing the first exercise several times to become familiar with the intervals in the I, IV, and V chords. Listen carefully to balance, tuning and blend.

Chord Drills:

- Build the first chord of each example from the bottom up or the top down. The director should dictate each chord. Singers can use staggered breathing and should listen carefully to balance, tuning, and blend. How does each part relate to the whole?
- Experiment with dynamics and singing the chords on different syllables. For example try Number 4 with the word "Al-le-lu-ia."
- Return to this page often, especially before sight-reading a song in F major.

Key Of F Exercises

Teaching Suggestions:

Concepts:

- Practice in the key of F
- Reinforce all previously learned rhythms, including:

  ♩. ♪

- Ties across bar lines

Directions:

- For each line, establish the starting pitch with the tonic chord and go!
- Sing each line twice through, once will be rough, and the second time will be for clean-up! Go right to the next line. Don't rehearse.
- On a different day, divide into parts, and sing the lines in any combination.
- Try some "catch me if you can" games in which a leader (teacher or student) starts singing a line and the others locate and join in.
- See how many different parts you can divide into without falling apart.
- Can the students come up with lyrics to fit any of the lines?

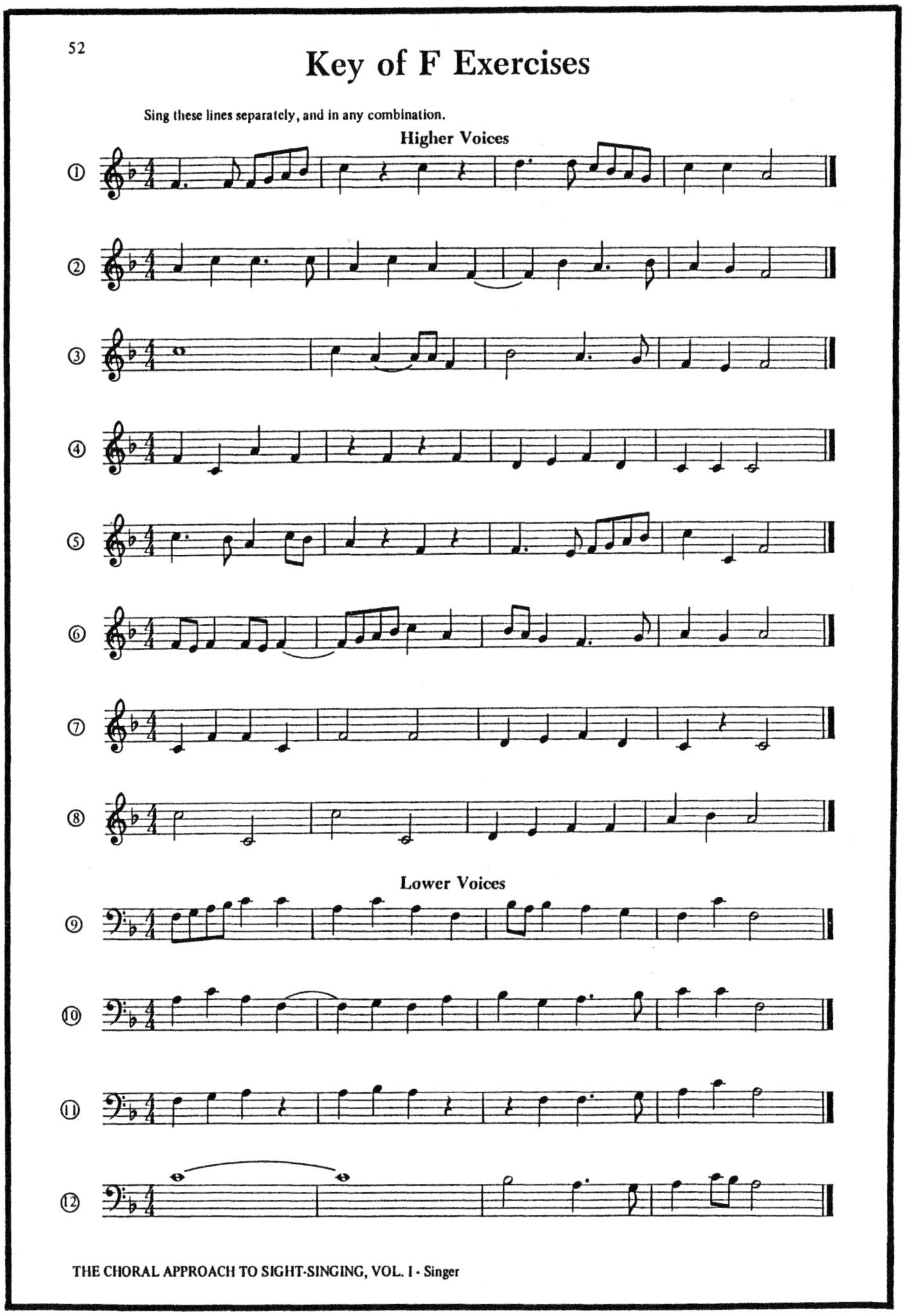

"Auld Lang Syne"

Teaching Suggestions:

Concepts:

- Key of F
- Pick-up note
- Slurs
- Dotted rhythms:

  ♩. ♪

- Half-step motion for Part II (ti-la-ti) and Part III (mi-fa-mi) which is difficult to keep in tune, and which is, by itself, somewhat boring. However, encourage the singers to listen to their part in relationship to the full harmony.
- Tonic to sub-dominant intervals in M. 8.

Directions:

- Isolate the potentially difficult intervals and caution the singers to listen carefully to help keep them in tune, especially if they include mi or ti.
- Point out the pick-up note.
- Establish the starting pitch and sight-read complete, skipping the usual steps, if possible.
- Repeat, so that the singers can correct their own errors.
- Did the boys notice that they only have 3 different pitches in the entire song?

"Old England"

Teaching Suggestions:

Concepts:

- Key of F
- $\frac{3}{4}$ Meter
- Review of dotted rhythms
- Ties, slurs
- Suspension (Part II)
- Skips within the I and V chords
- Featured section for Part III
- D. S. al Fine

Directions:

- Point out the D. S. al fine and explain what it means.
- Read on rhythm syllables throughout, noting the places where the notes are tied or slurred across the barline.
- Read on pitch syllables, parts together in rhythm.
- Establish the starting pitch and sing through, a cappella.
- Repeat so that the singers can correct their own mistakes, or if necessary, isolate the errors and correct them.
- Sing again with the text.
- Add the accompaniment.
- Add the dynamics.

NOTE: You may wish to point out the suspension in the Part II (M. 11-12 and M. 27-28) and have the students become aware of the "tension/release" quality that a suspension provides.

Perhaps one of the students could come up with another verse for "Old England" making it appropriate for performance.

55
far 'cross the sea. Sing me a song of Old
far 'cross the sea. Sing me a song of Old
far 'cross the sea. Sing me a song of Old
Fine
Eng - land. Old Eng - land's where I want to be.
Fine
Eng - land. Old Eng - land's where I want to be.
Fine
Eng - land. Old Eng - land's where I want to be.
Fine
THE CHORAL APPROACH TO SIGHT-SINGING, VOL. I - Singer

NOTES

NOTES

56
21
mf
Oh, 'Way, a - way!
Oh, 'Way, a - way!
f
I board - ed this ship on the sev - enth of June, 'twas
Oh, 'Way, a - way!
Oh, 'Way, a - way!
three years a - go to the day. I'm
THE CHORAL APPROACH TO SIGHT-SINGING, VOL. I - Singer

57
Oh, 'Way, a - way! To
Oh, 'Way, a - way! To
worn and I'm wear - y from sail - ing the seas. To
D.S. al Fine
Eng - land we're bound a - way. Oh!
Eng - land we're bound a - way. Oh!
Eng - land we're bound a - way. Oh!
D.S. al Fine
THE CHORAL APPROACH TO SIGHT-SINGING, VOL. I - Singer

NOTES

How To Find Do

Teaching Suggestions:

Concepts:

- Rule 1: Keys with no sharps or flats
- Rule 2: Flat keys
- Rule 3: Sharp keys

Directions:

- Use the board for explanations and examples.
- Read and discuss the rules as printed in the singer's edition.
- Practice with several examples on the board, and find other examples printed in their textbook or other choral pieces.

NOTE: You may use memory tricks to help remember the rules (for example "flat fa" or "sharp tack," but memorizing tables of key signatures may be demoralizing. Stress the usefulness of knowing how to find do on their own.

58

How To Find "Do"

You can find do in any key if you memorize the following three simple rules:

Rule 1: If there are no sharps (♯) or flats (♭) after the clef sign (𝄞 or 𝄢), do is automatically the key of C

Rule 2: If there are flats after the clef sign (key signature), the flat farthest to the right is fa. Count up or down to do.

Rule 3: If there are sharps in the key signature, the sharp farthest to the right is ti. Count up or down to do.

THE CHORAL APPROACH TO SIGHT-SINGING, VOL. I - Singer

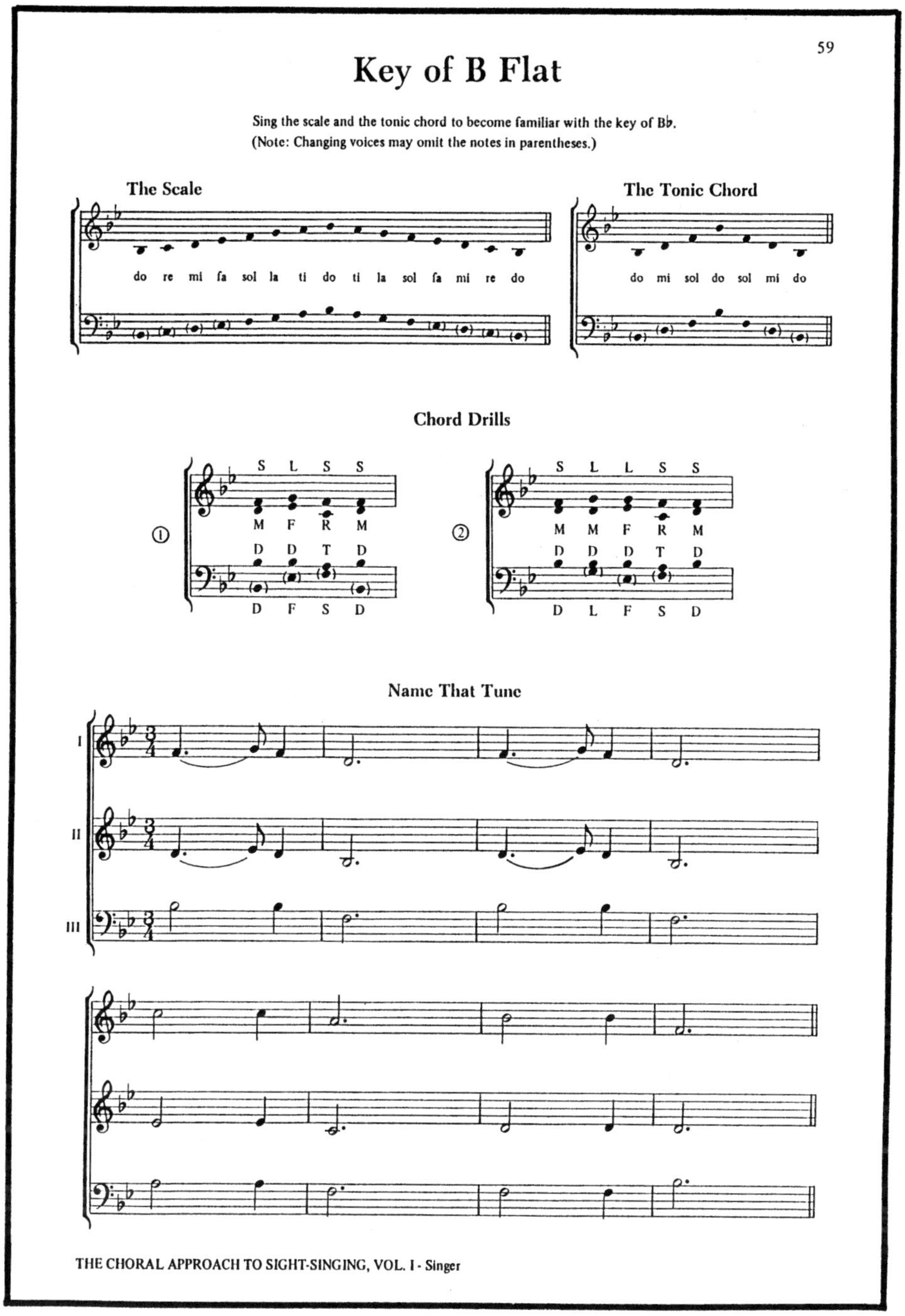

59

Key of B Flat

Sing the scale and the tonic chord to become familiar with the key of B♭.
(Note: Changing voices may omit the notes in parentheses.)

The Scale

do re mi fa sol la ti do ti la sol fa mi re do

The Tonic Chord

do mi sol do sol mi do

Chord Drills

① S L S S / M F R M / D D T D / D F S D

② S L L S S / M M F R M / D D D T D / D L F S D

Name That Tune

I II III

THE CHORAL APPROACH TO SIGHT-SINGING, VOL. I - Singer

Key Of B Flat

Teaching Suggestions:

Concepts:

- Introduce and practice the key of B flat.
- Dotted rhythms
- Slurs
- Name That Tune ("Silent Night" fragment)

Directions:

- Sing the scale and tonic chord several times to become familiar with the key of B flat. (Changed voices can sing the optional notes in parentheses.)
- Sing the chord drills, listening carefully for balance, tuning, and blend.
- NAME THAT TUNE: Look at the Part I melody. Can any student identify the song by singing silently?
- Have all students read the rhythm of Part I. Any guesses?
- Sight-read the Part I melody. Someone is sure to figure it out within the first four notes!
- Establish the starting pitches and sight-read parts together.

  Return to this page for review and reinforcement before sight-reading or rehearsing other songs in B flat.

Key Of D

Teaching Suggestions:

Concepts:

- Introduce and practice in the key of D
- Dotted rhythms
- Slurs
- Pick-up notes
- Name That Tune ("The First Noel" fragment)

Directions:

- Sing the scale and tonic chord several times to become familiar with the key of D.
- Sing the chord drills, listening carefully to balance, tuning and blend. Add the optional 4th (bass) part if you wish.
- Follow the usual procedures for playing NAME THAT TUNE.
- Review this page whenever you are sight-reading or rehearsing a song in the key of D.

Key Of A

Teaching Suggestions:

Concepts:

- Introduce and practice the key of A
- Name That Tune ("America" fragment)

Directions:

- Sing the scale and tonic chord in the key of A several times to become familiar with it.
- Sing the chord drills, listening carefully to balance, tuning, and blend.
- Play NAME THAT TUNE, following the usual procedure.
- Return to this page before sight-reading or rehearsing a song in the key of A.

Key Of E Flat

Teaching Suggestions:

Concepts:

- Introduce and practice the key of E flat.
- Name That Tune ("Deck The Halls" fragment)

Directions:

- Sing the scale and tonic chord several times to become familiar with the key of E flat.
- Sing the chord drills to help establish good intonation, balance, and blend.
- Play NAME THAT TUNE following the established procedures.
- Review this page before sight-reading or rehearsing a song in the key of E flat.

Key Of A Flat

Teaching Suggestions:

Concepts:

- Introduce and practice the key of A flat.
- Name That Tune ("Oh, Come All Ye Faithful" fragment)

Directions:

- Sing the scale and tonic chord a few times to become familiar with the key of A flat.
- Use the chord drills to help develop good intonation, balance, and blend.
- Play NAME THAT TUNE following the usual procedures.
- Review this page before sight-reading or rehearsing a song in the key of A flat.

Preview of Volume II

(Singer's Edition, p. 64)

Congratulations! If you have completed the songs and exercises in this book, you have taken the first steps toward becoming strong, self-confident sight-readers. You will find that you are able to apply your knowledge in other situations, and you will learn new songs faster and easier, without as much help from your teacher.

This is just the beginning, though. Sight-singing is a process which must be practiced often, as you refine your skills and add to them. If you move on into "The Choral Approach To Sight-Singing" Volume II, you will be practicing and reviewing all the concepts covered in Volume I, along with the following new concepts:

- More complete a cappella and accompanied songs (many with an optional 4th part for changed voices)
- More challenging rhythms (syncopation, sixteenth notes, more dotted rhythms, 6/8)
- More challenging melodic exercises (with bigger skips and more variety)
- Songs and exercises using accidentals
- Songs and exercises using minor keys
- Minor key chord progressions
- Introduction to songs with modulations

And much more!!!

About The Authors

EMILY HOLT CROCKER is a native Texan and was a professional music educator for fifteen years. She taught all levels of choral music, specializing in middle school/junior high, where her choirs received numerous superior ratings in concert and sight-reading competitions. In 1989, she joined the music publishing industry and now holds the position of Senior Choral Editor at Hal Leonard Publishing Corporation.

She has received degrees from the University of North Texas and Texas Women's University and has done additional post-graduate work at UNT where she was assistant conductor of the A Cappella Choir and taught elementary music education classes.

Emily is a frequent clinician, adjudicator, and guest conductor and has over a hundred published works for choir.

JOYCE EILERS' compositions are consistent favorites of teachers and students across the nation, and while her teaching experience spans all levels, she is particularly well-known for her work with elementary and junior high singers. Because she is so aware of the special needs and limitations of young singers, her music always places strong emphasis on techniques that have been tested and proven through her own experience in the classroom.

Joyce received her undergraduate degree from the Oklahoma City University and her masters degree from the University of Oregon. She now devotes herself to a full-time composing career and writes exclusively for Hal Leonard Publishing Corporation.

Let us hear from you!

We'd love to hear how this method worked for you. Write to us at:

Hal Leonard Publishing Corporation
Attn: The Choral Approach To Sight-Singing
7777 W. Bluemound Rd.
Milwaukee, WI 53213

TERMS AND SYMBOLS

I. **DYNAMICS** (loudness and softness)

pp - (pianissimo) (pee-ah-NEE-see-moh) - very soft
p - (piano) (pee-AH-noh) - soft
mp - (mezzo piano) (MEH-tsoh) - medium soft
mf - (mezzo forte) - medium loud
f - (forte) (FOR-teh) - loud
ff - (fortissimo) (for-TEE-see-moh) - very loud

crescendo (*cresc.* <) (kreh-SHEN-doh) - gradually louder

decrescendo (*decresc.* >) (deh-kreh-SHEN-doh) - gradually softer

diminuendo (*dim.*) (dih-min-new-EN-doh) - gradually softer

accent (♩>) - stress the note by singing it louder.

II. **TEMPO** (TEM-poh) - the speed of the beat

accellerando (*accel.*) (ah-chel-leh-RAHN-doh) - gradually faster

rallentando (*rall.*) (rahl-en-TAHN-doh) - gradually slower

ritardando (*rit.* or *ritard.*) (ree-tahr-DAHN-doh) - gradually slower

fermata 𝄐 (fur-MAH-tah) - hold the note for longer than its value; the length is left up to the interpretation of the director.

metronome marking (♩= 100) - a marking which appears over the first staff of music which indicates the kind of note which will get the beat, and the number of beats per minute as measured by a metronome.

rubato (roo-BAH-toh) - the tempo is free; left up to the interpretation of the director

style word - a marking which appears over the first staff of music, which indicates either the tempo or the way (style) the music is to be sung.

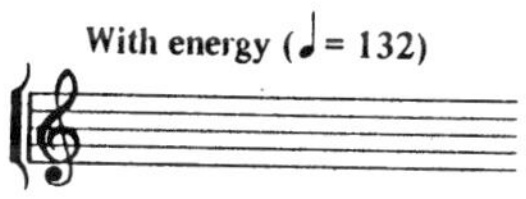

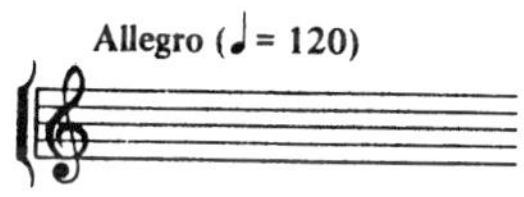

Largo (LAHR-goh) - very slow
Adagio (ah-DAH-jee-oh) - slow
Andante (ahn-DAHN-teh) - medium
Moderato (mah-deh-RAH-toh) - medium
Allegro (ah-LEH-groh) -fast
Vivace (vee-VA-cheh) - very fast
Presto (PREH-stoh) - very fast

A Tempo (ah TEM-poh) - return to the original tempo (speed)

III. **OTHER TERMS AND SYMBOLS**

coda (KOH-dah) - ending

Da capo (D. C.) (dah KAH-poh) - repeat from the beginning

D.C. al fine (ahl-FEE-neh) - repeat from the beginning to "fine" (end)

Dal Segno (D.S.) (dahl SAYN-yoh) - go back to the sign 𝄋 and repeat

D.S. al fine (ahl FEE-neh) - repeat from the sign 𝄋 to "fine" (end)

divisi (*div.*) (dee-VEE-see) - divide, the part divides

legato (leh-GAH-toh) - smoothly connected, may be connected by a slur

molto (MOHL-toh) - much, very (molto rit.)

poco (POH-koh) - little (poco cresc.)

repeat - 𝄆 𝄇 repeat the section. If the first repeat sign is omitted, go back to the beginning

First and Second Endings: At the end of the first ending (bracket 1), repeat, but skip the first ending and go to the second ending (bracket 2).

sempre (SEHM-preh) - always and the next time through ex; sempre forte = always loud.

simile (SIM-eh-leh) - continue in the same way

staccato (♩) (stah-KAH-toh) - short, separated notes

’ - take a breath

n.b. (no breath) and ◠ (dotted slur) - Do not breathe here

IV. PITCH

Ex. 1

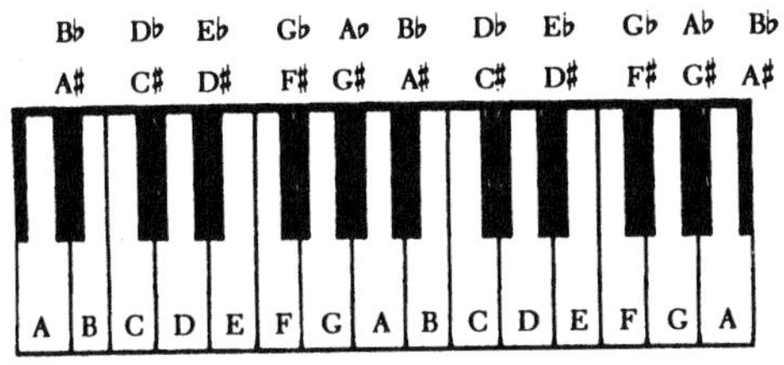

Ex. 2

Ex. 3

V. SYLLABLES

MOVABLE DO

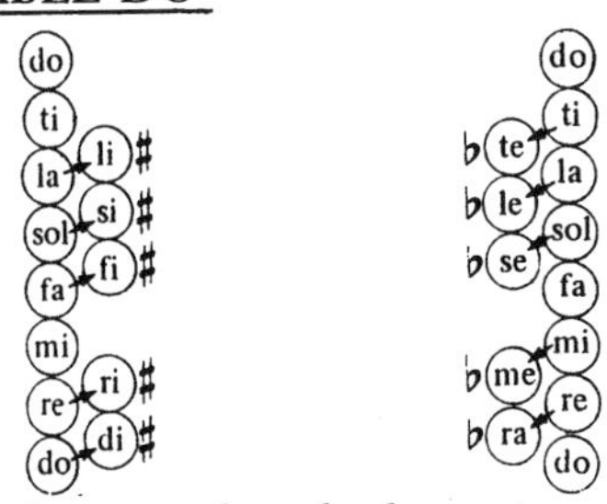

In movable do, do is designated as the home tone (or tonic) in every key.

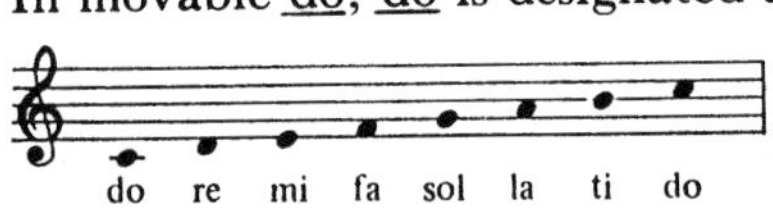

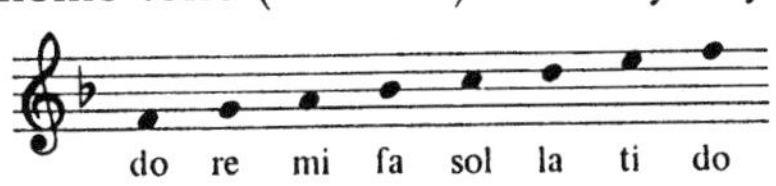

PATTERNS OF SOUND has been written using movable do.

FIXED DO

In fixed do, C is always do, no matter what the key.

Ex. 1

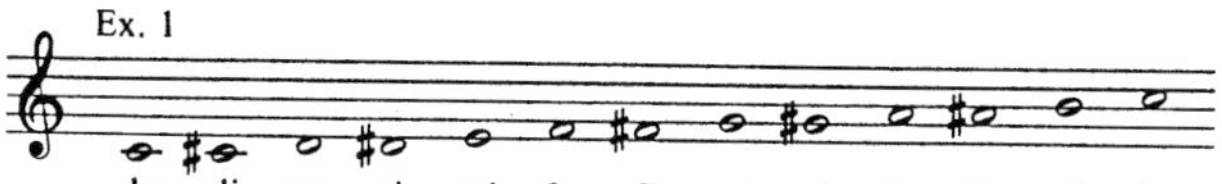

Ex. 2

In fixed do, keys other than C retain their fixed location, and use the altered pitch syllables.

NUMBERS

Numbers can be used instead of the syllables in movable do.

do	=	8
ti	=	7
la	=	6
sol	=	5
fa	=	4
mi	=	3
re	=	2
do	=	1

VI. **RHYTHM** - the organization of non-pitched sounds in time

(ta) - quarter note — quarter rest

(ta-a) - half note — half rest

(ta-a-a) - dotted half note — dotted half rest

(ta-a-a-a) - whole note — whole rest (may also refer to an empty measure)

ti ti (or ti ti) - eighth notes — eighth rest

ti ki ti ki (or ti ki ti ki) - sixteenth notes — sixteenth rest

Dots - a dot lengthens a note by half its value

VII. **METER** - Meter refers to the grouping of beats.

A meter signature or time signature indicates the grouping with two numbers:

$$\begin{matrix}4\\4\end{matrix}\qquad\begin{matrix}3\\4\end{matrix}\qquad\begin{matrix}2\\4\end{matrix}\qquad\begin{matrix}6\\8\end{matrix}$$

The top number indicates the number of beats per measure and the bottom number indicates the kind of note getting the beat.

GLOSSARY

Absolute Pitch - The letter names of the notes (see PITCH, p. 68).

A Cappella - (ah-kah-PEH-lah) Singing without instrumental accompaniment.

Accent - Stress of emphasize a note by singing it louder.

Accidentals - Symbols that move the pitch up or down a half step.

♯ - sharp - raises the pitch one half step

♭ - flat - lowers the pitch one half step

♮ - natural - cancels a previous sharp or flat. (When it cancels a flat, the pitch is raised one half step; when it cancels a sharp, the pitch is lowered one half step).

Accidentals affect all notes of the same pitch that follow the accidental within the same measure, or if an altered note is tied over a barline.

Bar - See measure.

Barline - A vertical line to separate measures. A double bar indicates the end of a song.

Barline

Double Bar

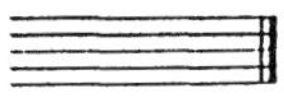

Beat - The unit of pulse in music.

Chord - Three or more pitches sounding at the same time or in a pitch ladder (broken chord). Common chords used at this level include:

Numerous other examples are built on other scale steps, or involve accidentals, and will become more common as you gain sight-reading competency.

Chromatic - Moving up or down by half steps (See PITCH, p. 68).

Clef - The symbol at the beginning of the staff.

TREBLE CLEF
Used for higher voices and instruments, and the piano right hand. The curve is wrapped around the G, so it is also called the G clef.

BASS CLEF
Used for lower voices and instruments and the piano left hand. The two dots are on either side of F, so it is often referred to as the F clef.

Coda - See OTHER TERMS AND SYMBOLS, p. 67

Common Time - 4/4 meter indicated in the time signature with the symbol "C".

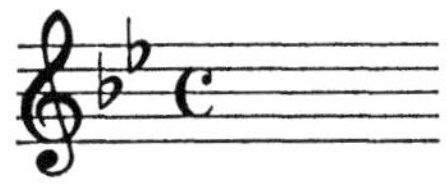

Cut Time - Technically it is 2/2 time, but it is really 4/4 time where the half note gets the beat. It is marked with the symbol ₵ (common time cut in half).

Da Capo - See OTHER TERMS AND SYMBOLS, p. 67

Dal Segno - See OTHER TERMS AND SYMBOLS, p. 67

Diatonic - Step by step movement within a regular scale (any key).

Divisi - *(div.)* Divide, the part divides.

Downbeat - The (accented) first beat of the measure.

Enharmonic - Notes with more than one name. For instance, F♯ and G♭ are the same note, they are "enharmonic" with each other. Di and ra are enharmonic, etc.

Fermata - See TEMPO, p.

Fine - See OTHER TERMS AND SYMBOLS, p.

Flat - ♭ See ACCIDENTALS. Flat also refers to faulty intonation, when the notes are sung or played slightly under the correct pitch.

G Clef - 𝄞 See CLEF, p. 70

Half Step - The interval between notes of a chromatic scale. (do - di, re - ri, etc. and F - F♯, A♭ - G, etc.)

Harmony - Two or more musical tones sounding at the same time.

Interval - The distance between two pitches.

Intonation - Accuracy of pitch.

Key - The organization of tonality around a single pitch (key-note). Scales have relationships between scale steps that remain constant even when the key-note moves. In solfege, the key-note is do in major and la in minor (see KEY-NOTE AND KEY SIGNATURE).

Key-Note - The pitch which is the tonal center of a key. The first tone (degree) of a scale. It is also called the "tonic." A key is named after the key-note; for example in the key of A♭, A♭ is the key-note. (See KEY AND KEY SIGNATURE).

Key Signature - The group of sharps or flats at the beginning of a staff which combine to indicate the locations of the key-note. If there are no sharps or flats, the key is automatically C major or A minor, and do is located:

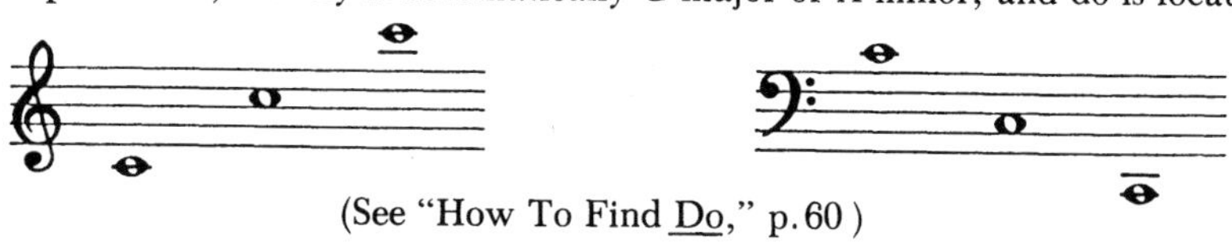

(See "How To Find Do," p. 60)

Legato - See OTHER TERMS AND SYMBOLS, p. 68

Ledger Lines - The short lines used to extend the lines and spaces of the staff. (Sometimes spelled "leger" lines)

Major Key/Scale/Mode - A tonality in which the key-note is do and the half and whole step pattern of the scale is:

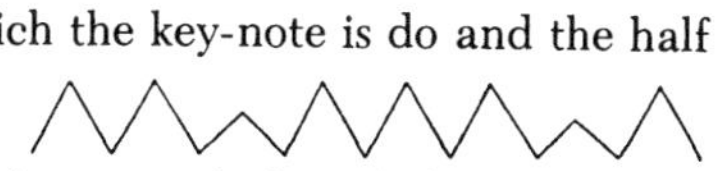

do re mi fa sol la ti do
1 2 3 4 5 6 7 8
half step half step

Measure - A group of beats divided by barlines. Measures are sometimes called bars. The first beat of each measure is accented.

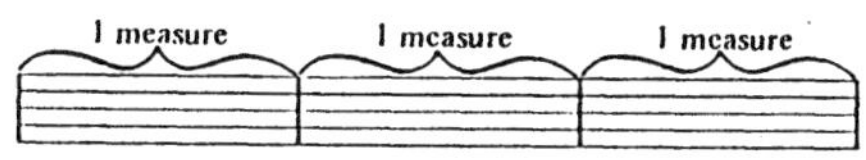

Melody - A succession of musical tones; also the predominant line in a song.

Meter - The grouping of beats. (See METER, p. 69)

Meter Signature - See METER, p. 69)

Middle C - The C which is located closest to the middle of the piano keyboard. Middle C can be written in either treble or bass clef.

These two notes are enharmonic (same note) (see enharmonic)

Minor Key/Mode/Scale - A tonality in which the key-note is la, and the half/whole step pattern of the scale is:

la ti do re mi fa sol la
1 2 3 4 5 6 7 8
half step half step

Accidentals are frequently used in a minor key, most often after fi and si.

Modulation - Changing keys in the middle of a song. Adjust to the key signature, the key-note, and proceed.

Natural - See ACCIDENTALS, p. 70)

Notation - All written notes and symbols which are used to represent music.

Octave - The interval between two notes of the same name:

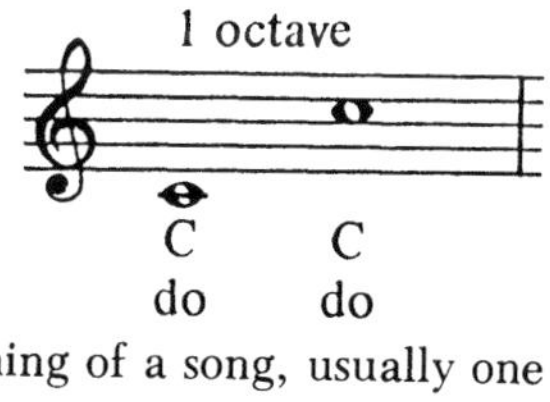

Pick-Up - An incomplete measure at the beginning of a song, usually one or two notes. The last measure should be correspondingly shorter.

Pitch - The highness or lowness of musical sounds.

Pitch Ladder - See TONIC CHORD, p. 72

Relative Major/Minor - Major and minor tonalities which share the same key signature.

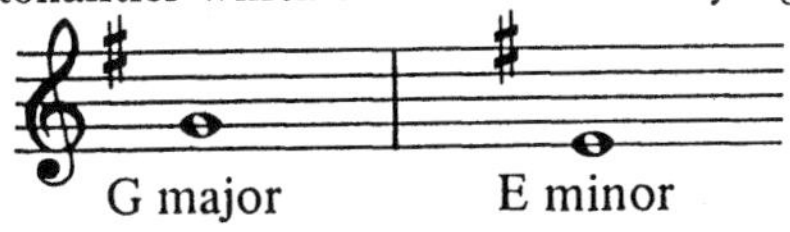

Repeat - See OTHER TERMS AND SYMBOLS, p. 68

Rhythm - The organization of non-pitched sounds in time. (To avoid confusion, beat is "the steady pulse in music," while rhythm is "the way the words go.")

Scale - An arrangement of successive pitches in a set order or pattern to indicate tonality.

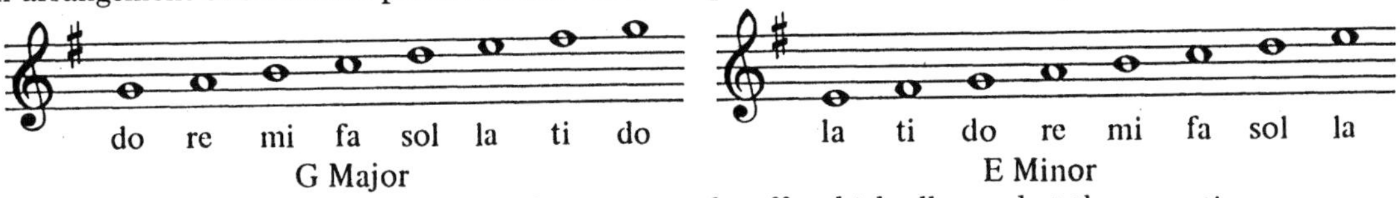

Score - The arrangement of a group of vocal and instrumental staffs which all sound at the same time.

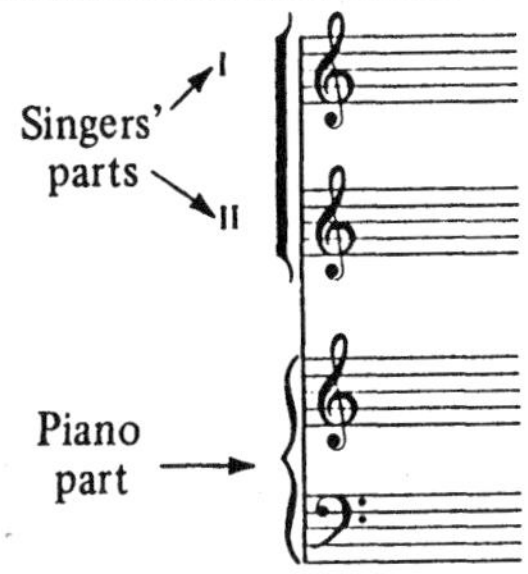

Sequence - The successive repetition of a short melodic idea at different pitch levels.

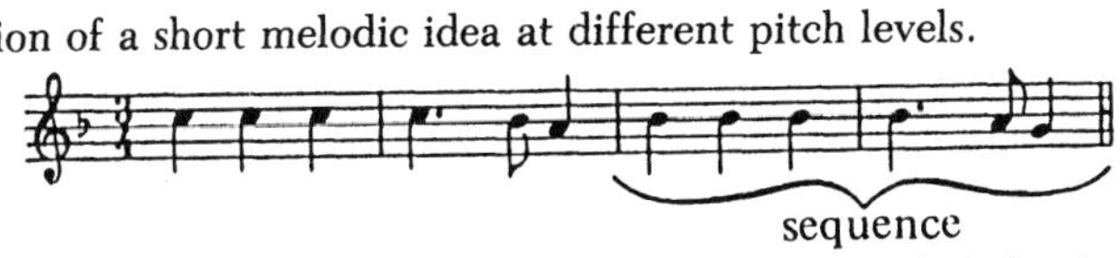

Sharp - ♯ See ACCIDENTALS; also, faulty intonation in which the note is sung slightly above the correct pitch.

Skip - The melodic movement of one note to another in intervals larger than a step.

Slur - See p. 42

Solfege (sohl-FEZH) or solfeggio (sohl-FEJ-ee-oh) - The study of sight-singing using pitch syllables (do re mi, etc.)

Staccato - See OTHER TERMS AND SYMBOLS, p. 68

Staff - The five horizontal parallel lines on which notes are placed to show pitch.

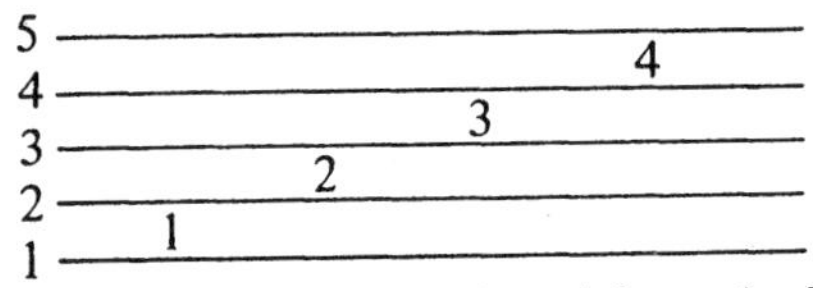

The lines and spaces are numbered from the bottom up.

Step - Melodic movement from one note to the next higher or lower scale degree.

Syllables - Names given to pitch units or rhythm units to aid in sight-reading.

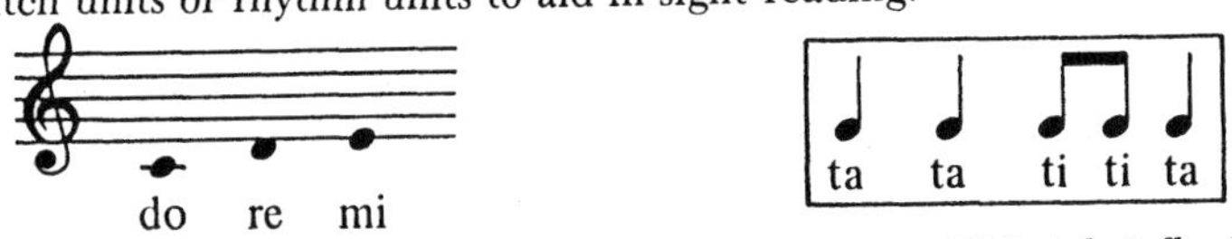

Syncopation - The use of accents in irregular places to create rhythmic interest. This is briefly discussed on p. . Other examples include:

Tempo - See TEMPO, p.

Tie - See p. 40

Time Signature - See METER, p. 69

Tonality - The organization of pitches in a song in which a certain pitch (tone) is designated as the "key-note" or the note which is the tonal center of a key.

Tone - A musical sound of definite pitch and quality.

Tonic - The key-note of a key or scale.

Tonic Chord - The name given to the chord built on the key-note of the scale (pitch ladder).

Transpose - To re-write or perform a song in a key other than the original.

Treble Clef - 𝄞 See CLEF, p. 70

Triad - See CHORD, p. 70

Triplet - Three notes of the same value which are equal in duration to two notes of the same value.

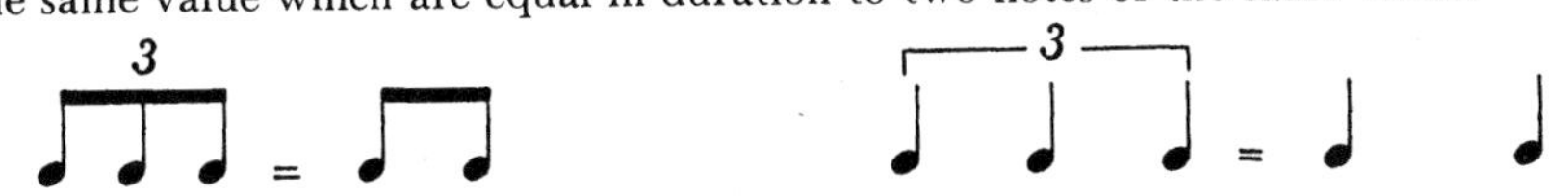

Unison - All parts singing the same notes at the same time, (or singing in octaves).

Whole Step - Two half steps.